Slater, Philip
Elliot.

Wealth addiction

Wealth Addiction

Also by Philip Slater

MICROCOSM □ THE GLORY OF HERA

THE PURSUIT OF LONELINESS □ EARTHWALK

FOOTHOLDS □ THE WAYWARD GATE

Wealth Addiction

PHILIP SLATER

E. P. DUTTON • NEW YORK

For information contact:
E.P. Dutton, 2 Park Avenue, New York, N.Y. 10016

Library of Congress Cataloging in Publication Data
Slater, Philip Elliot.
Wealth addiction.

Includes bibliographical references.
1. Wealth, Ethics of. I. Title.
HB835.S65 1980   179′.8   79-16370
ISBN: 0-525-23073-4

Published simultaneously in Canada by Clarke, Irwin & Company Limited, Toronto and Vancouver

Designed by Barbara Huntley

10 9 8 7 6 5 4 3 2 1

First Edition

*Since olden times there has rarely been
a sage who was wealthy.*
YOSHIDA KENKŌ

*Wealth is like muck.
It is not good but if it be spread.*
SIR FRANCIS BACON

Contents

Acknowledgments

Writing this book was a struggle which would have been difficult to win through without the help of others. Melita Cowie was the source of many ideas and much inspiration. The support of my Men's Group, to whom this book is dedicated, was important throughout. The vigilant editorial eye of Bill Whitehead curbed many excesses, and his wisdom was, as always, invaluable. Chuck Gibson was an early, responsive, and helpful critic. And Elna Sandeman's intelligent handling of the manuscript's preparation relieved me of many burdens.

An altered version of Chapter 2 appeared in *Quest 77,* while parts of Chapters 3 and 5 appeared in *Social Policy* (September, 1978). Most of the epigraphs were culled from Goldian VandenBroeck's *Less Is More.*

Wealth Addiction

1

What Is Money?

I saw clearly,
that there was a real valuableness
in all the common things;
in the scarce, a feigned.
THOMAS TRAHERNE

People worry a lot about money these days. In a way this is peculiar, since the money is worth less than ever before. We try harder and harder to make more and more money, which buys less and less. A visitor from outer space might expect that if money were decreasing in value we'd stop being so interested in it. Why worry about something that's on its way to becoming worthless?

One reason we're so preoccupied with money is that we've confused it with survival, although it has no nutritional value, is poor building material, and won't keep us warm. Yet we have become psychologically so dependent on it that most of us have a hard time even imagining survival apart from money. For many people, of course—especially city dwellers—survival in the absence of money presents real difficulties. If enough people believe something, they can create a world that makes those beliefs come true, and we've pretty much done that with money. We can, by the same token, try out some new beliefs and create a new kind of world—one in which all our present

1

beliefs about money will seem completely irrational. This book is an effort in that direction.

When we step back far enough to get a good look at them, some of our beliefs about money already seem pretty irrational. This is what gives us the leverage to start creating a new belief system for ourselves. In fact, our society has a peculiarly split personality right now: one part cautiously exploring new directions while the other pushes the old approach to its wildest extremes. This is what usually happens during periods of change.

Pushing old patterns to an extreme is one way to describe the rush of "success" books that have flooded the market in the past few years. These books purport to show you how to make a million dollars on or off the stock market (never what to do with the money when you get it, which almost everyone mistakenly assumes he or she already knows) or how to trap yourself irrevocably in the "rat race" by rising to the top of a corporation.

In almost all these books money is the ultimate value against which everything else is measured. Rarely, if ever, is it put in the larger context of what people want out of life and what kind of society they want to live in. Money, of course, has its own logic, its own rules for maximizing itself. This is what economics is all about. The basic rules are simple, but the applications and ramifications can be quite elaborate. Sometimes people get so caught up in these rules they begin to confuse them with their own goals. Money rules, for example, tell us how to maximize our bank balance, assuming, quite contrary to the facts, that we all *want* to maximize our bank balances. Of course if you ask people, "Do you want to make a lot of money?" they'll say yes. But to achieve this end they are rarely willing to sacrifice all other goals and values: to accumulate paper, or enlarge the number of digits in a computer is not the ultimate goal that most people live for. They want to enjoy themselves, be comfortable, have adventures, get good at what they do, grow and develop, love and be loved, make the world better, and so on. A big bank balance can be useful at times in realizing some of these goals, but it can be an actual detriment to the attainment of others. The "How To" books are quite correct, however, in saying that *anyone willing to dispense with all these other goals can make money.*

The way of looking at the world that makes maximizing money a paramount goal I call *Moneythink.* If you buy something you don't want because you think it will increase in money value, you're operating on Moneythink. If you sell something you *do* want because it's going to decrease in value, you're also engaged in Moneythink. Anytime you do anything with the goal of making money you use Moneythink. The field of economics is based on Moneythink. The financial pages of the newspaper and the books about how to be "successful" are all expressions of Moneythink.

As a means of achieving a limited and temporary goal Moneythink is very useful. But in our society many people have a tendency to arrange their lives around it. If you want to learn how to sail a boat, it's very useful to read a book giving you rules and principles of sailing. But you wouldn't apply those rules to your entire life. You'd look awfully silly if you walked down the street tacking back and forth against the wind, and if you did it in your car you'd be arrested.

If we are to understand money without being swallowed up in Moneythink—if we are to learn why money has such a hold on us, and how to keep it in its proper place as a tool that we use rather than an obsession that uses us—then we need to appreciate three important facts about money:

1. It is symbolic, not real.
2. Its function is to homogenize.
3. It is a means, not an end.

It's hard to talk about these things without stating the obvious, but where money is concerned, the obvious is usually the first thing forgotten, especially by those who are supposed to know the most about it.

MONEY IS SYMBOLIC

When I say money is symbolic I mean that it has value only as long as we collectively believe that it does. Inflation, for example, which I'll discuss in more detail in Chapter 6, could be considered a sign of incipient skepticism. We might say that the 70's raised the same doubts about money that the eighteenth century raised about religion. Money is like the fairies in *Peter Pan*: if you stop believing in it, it sickens and dies. Fortunately, many Americans are incurable romantics—the sicker the money gets, the harder they work to keep it alive.

As we all know, money came into being to make barter more efficient, at a time when transportation and communications were in a very primitive state. Labor is needed in April, a crop is harvested in September, a ship comes into harbor in January—how can these complex exchanges be managed? Money makes trade more elastic: in effect it's an elaborate system of I.O.U.s. It has the advantage that while one person's I.O.U. may turn out to be worthless, money becomes worthless only when large numbers of us stop believing in it. It's a *collective* I.O.U.

But in a mere few thousand years these symbols have become very concrete in people's minds. To most Americans, in fact, money is the realest thing imaginable, and people who pride themselves on being down-to-earth and materialistic will focus all their interest and energies on a complete intangible. The Texas oil billionaire H. L. Hunt, once thought to be the richest man alive, was quoted as saying, "Money is nothing. It's just something to make bookkeeping convenient." Yet he devoted his life to the accumulation of this "nothing." Because money is the symbol for acquiring many goods and services, it assumes for many people the character of a magic wishing ring—the gateway to all our desires. People actually work to amass these I.O.U.s before they have even considered what they want them for.

I once conducted several workshops for people who wanted to explore their attitudes and feelings about money. I designed games and exercises to make these explorations more concrete. I created a mini-economy, for example, complete with markets, wages, and so on, and a game in which people responded to comments they liked by giving the speaker chips. One result always fascinated me: once a piece of paper, or any other worthless object, has been treated as money, many people have a hard time letting go of this association.

Suppose, for example, I tear up and distribute some little pieces of paper for people to use in purchasing small amounts of food or minor services. Suppose, further, that after this has been going on for some time I suddenly announce that in five minutes the pieces of paper can no longer be used to purchase anything. You'd expect that everyone would try as quickly as possible to use up this "money" that's about to become worthless—this, after all, is what happens in an inflation panic. It happens here, too, but more slowly than one would expect. I have repeatedly seen people cling to fistfuls of worthless paper as enthusiastically as if they were ten-dollar bills. It's very easy to attach value to a symbol, but much more difficult to take it away again. This seems to be what has happened to money itself.

Actually, money is less needed now than at any time in modern history. With improvements in transportation, communication, and information storage, direct barter becomes much easier and is, in fact, occurring on an increasing scale. Most goods can be delivered anywhere in the world in a matter of weeks. Communication is instantaneous. And debts and credits can be stored in a computer indefinitely. This is really all that is needed to restore barter to an important place in the world economy, and as inflation lowers our faith in money, barter will play an increasing role at the corporate level. Barter is also becoming important at the personal level, among the "voluntary poor"—middle-class people who have adopted a simpler life-style. People in these networks frequently exchange services on a regular basis—particularly those with skills in carpentry, arts and crafts, various kinds of healing, car repair, building, and information.

MONEY HOMOGENIZES

Money is useful to us only to the degree that it creates a *single standard of value.* If it didn't have this ability to homogenize value, money would be pointless.

We attach different kinds of meaning to our experiences and don't usually try to compare or equate them. We don't say, "This sunset is worth three sets of tennis, one episode of 'Starsky and Hutch', and a banana split." Each experience produces not only a *degree* of pleasure, but a certain *kind* of pleasure, with special meanings attached. A grapefruit is not only *quantitatively* different from a grape in the sense of being bigger, but also *qualitatively* different: it has a different taste, texture, and so on. Money was created to enable us to eliminate these qualitative differences and compare anything with anything else on a single scale of value. There's an old saying about the folly of trying to compare apples and oranges, but this is precisely what money is for: if apples are 10¢ each and oranges are 20¢ each, then an orange is twice as good as an apple. This doesn't tell us much about the difference between *experiencing* an orange and an apple but it's extremely convenient in the marketplace.

Reducing all things to one common scale of value makes it much easier to trade them. But if you invent something to kill pests, it has a tendency to kill other things too; and if you invent something to homogenize traded goods, it tends to homogenize everything. Suppose we meet an alien to this planet and teach him all about money—and nothing else. We tell him that oranges are worth twice as much as apples and give him enough money to have all he wants of both. On the basis of this information he would never taste an apple, unless he had some whimsical curiosity about what an inferior experience might be like. Money is not concerned with the unique qualities of experience.

A distinguished physicist once expressed to me his amazement that there was only one *kind* of money—that all aspects of living could be compressed into a single quantitative scale of value. This is the great strength of money: it can reduce so much to so little. This is also its greatest weakness.

Some things, it's true, are felt by most people to lie outside this single scale: aesthetic experiences, emotions, sexual feelings, religious and ideological convictions, and so on. Art is bought and sold, however, and so, to some extent, are sexual gratification, companionship, nurturance, devotion, and other emotion-laden experiences. Most of the major world religions began by praising poverty, but institutions need money to enhance themselves and many existing churches have severely compromised this view. Jesus of Nazareth, for example, taught that poverty was blessed and that a rich man would be automatically excluded from heaven; yet some Christian denominations have gone so far as openly to equate wealth with virtue.

We also claim that we cannot place a value on human life, yet we do it all the time. In wartime the loss of lives is weighed quite explicitly against the loss of equipment. The neutron bomb involves detailed calculations of the dollar worth of human beings relative to real estate. Manufacturers of safety equipment, road builders, automobile and airplane manufacturers, hospitals, drug, food, cosmetic, and pesticide manufacturers and processors are all involved in calculations in which the probability of death (and its cost in lawsuits, etc.) is weighed against the expense of ensuring against that death. If the expense is too great, a higher probability of death is tolerated.

The price of human life was recently made even more explicit in a research study conducted by a psychologist, Paul Cameron. On the assumption that they would not be found out, nearly half of a sample of subjects who had killed before (in the army, for example) said they would kill again, for an average minimum price of $20,000. Of those who had never killed anyone before, far fewer said they would be willing to do it now, and those who did would demand a higher price: $50,-000. (One of the benefits of war, apparently, is that it not only increases the supply of hit men, but also lowers their fee.)

Money, then, is like a government agency—continually trying to enlarge its jurisdiction. Just as TV, which exists for the purpose of entertaining us, tends to convert everything into entertainment, even the news, so money, which exists to create a common standard of value, tends to reduce everything to that standard, even life and death.

This is very handy in the supermarket but creates some problems for us as human beings. If everything in my life can be compared with everything else along a single standard, then my choices are very simple and I could easily be replaced by a computer. Money, in other words, mechanizes motivation. This is important to remember: *if the purposes for which money was designed were fulfilled completely, there would be no reason for humans to exist as decision-making beings;* we could all just bliss out and leave the business of living in the world to robots, who would create a completely rational economy that would be stable for eternity. This may seem like a silly statement to make, but it reflects the ideal model that most economists carry in the backs of their heads, and the direction in which we are continually being pushed by our relationship to money and the attitudes of "experts."

But this isn't all. The moment I begin to compare all my needs on a single scale I'm overwhelmed with information about my priorities. Do I really *want* to know that going to a good movie has a higher priority for me than giving money to any number of worthy causes? If we were open about money, this single standard would lay bare all our selfishness, our stinginess, our compulsions. A completely detailed budget, analyzed and interpreted, would reveal the relative strength of most of our impulses and desires. Imagine the domestic quarrels that would follow the exposure of a complete rank-ordered budget—the embarrassment! A man might get away with saying to his wife that "we can't afford new shoes for the children"—but he'd never get away with "my two martinis at the commuter bar every night are more important than the children's feet." As it is, most couples confront each other now and then: "If we can afford X, why can't we afford Y?" or "If you can spend all that on *your* clothes, then I'm going to spend some on *mine.*" But such arguments are haphazard and piece-meal—full disclosure would multiply them drastically, which is no doubt why people are so prudish about their private money affairs. Generally, if I don't want to look at the fact that I care more about my pleasure than your food, I'll blur this by saying "I can't afford your food." Then instead of dealing with my priorities I've converted the problem into needing more money, so I can have my pleasure and give you your food and I won't feel guilty anymore. Multiply this decision by a thousand and you have the life condition of the average middle-class American.

MONEY IS A MEANS

Whenever we use the words "I can't afford it," we're giving away part of our humanity. We're abdicating all responsibility for our desires and all our power to make choices, and surrendering that power and that responsibility to money, which, as we've already observed, is an empty symbol. Instead of standing up like an adult and saying honestly "I'd rather drink than eat," or "I'd rather have a TV than enough clothes to wear," or "I care more about feeding my family than owning a car," or "I don't want to go to Europe enough to give up going to movies for two years," we play the dependent child and say "Oh, I really *want* to, but Daddy Money won't let me." We're not willing to stand behind our own motivations. We deny our power to choose and give it away to money.

The above thoughts are addressed primarily to people who have enough money to make at least a few choices about how it is spent. But what about a person who is really poor? Isn't it reasonable for such a person to say "I can't afford it"? (People say "I can't afford it" whether they make $5,000 a year or $500,000 a year.) People living in abject poverty have better things to think about than linguistic subtleties. But the principle still holds: "I can't afford it" in that case means "I don't want it enough to steal it."

For a middle-class person, saying "I can't afford it" leads by subtle steps to the conversion of money from a means to an end. Money, after all, is only a tool, as we've all been taught. Logically, then, we would never think about money until we knew what it was we wanted it for. Saying "I can't afford it" blurs this distinction between means and ends. We start thinking "I need money for a number of things I think I want." Soon this becomes "I need money." We've completely lost sight of the ends for which money was the means. Before money existed we knew we needed food, or shelter, or an ax. Now we don't know what we need. We say we need money. Sometimes this is a shorthand way of saying "I need several things that I don't want to bore you by telling you about" or "I'm in debt to people." But often it describes accurately a set of feelings people have, a felt need. Such cases should arouse our sympathy, for while money can be the *means* for satisfying certain human needs, in and of itself it can satisfy no need.

We can see how confused people have become by looking at a common piece of American behavior: a man or woman sits at home clutching a fistful of these collective I.O.U.s and leafs through a catalog, looking for something to buy. Having decided "I need money" (which either means "I need money *for such-and-such*" or is a symptom of mental derangement), I now have to consult a book to discover what I needed it *for!* When we "go shopping" without a clear goal in mind, means and ends have become reversed. Instead of acquiring money to help us get something we need, we buy something we don't need to help us spend the money we acquired.

Money, then, twists our thinking and puts us out of touch with our fundamental goals and desires. Instead of using money to serve ourselves, we use ourselves to serve money. This is what people mean when they say Americans "worship money."

It isn't only at the individual level that this confusion occurs. When politicians, business leaders, and economists talk about money they say we should do this or that in order to increase corporate or personal income or the availability of jobs, as if these were ends. But money and jobs merely channel human energy and time into some activity, toward some goal, and the goal is never stated. We talk continually about *how to produce the tools to perform a task that has never been specified.* Generating work and money have become ends in themselves—what the task is seems to be unimportant so long as the work and spending continue. We rarely ask what we as Americans want to do with our time and energy and resources.

We often hear these money experts talk about "economic feasibility" and whether a given course of action is "economically justified." This is the same old "can't-afford-it" confusion of ends and means on a national scale. How do we know what is "feasible" until we know what we want and how much we want it? "Not economically feasible" or "not economically justified" means simply that "we don't want that as much as we want some other things." Politically it's a lot easier to say "smog-reducing measures are not economically feasible" than to say "we'd rather let 10,000 people die of emphysema than reduce the profits of polluting corporations."

Many dubious activities in our society—for example, manufacturing poisons or destroying the environment in various ways—are justified on the grounds that they create jobs for people. But why would someone want to work at a monotonous and soul-eating assembly-line job producing something unnecessary or dangerous or destructive? (After all, heroin also creates jobs for people and the work is more interesting.) The answer always given is that people need money. For what? There is enough food, clothing, and shelter for all our people, though it is poorly distributed: many have more than they use; others less than they need. Meanwhile, vast land and energy resources are devoted to products that are unnourishing, unhealthy, and useless. For the most part people need money to spend on things that we have spent billions persuading ourselves we need. In short, we need unnecessary jobs so that people will have unnecessary money to buy unnecessary things. And we need to buy unnecessary things in order to create unnecessary jobs so that people will have unnecessary money. I recently saw an article in a paper stating that the American people were "economically illiterate" and needed to be "educated" by business leaders and economists so that they would understand that this system is completely rational and works for their own good.

Sometimes when I listen to government and business experts talk about money I have a vision of people frantically preparing themselves for a journey. They argue about what clothes to take, what mode of transportation would be best, what maps and guides to use. They buy skis, scuba gear, mountain-climbing equipment. They buy plane tickets, tune up the car, paint their boat. They argue about which of the things they're doing is the best preparation for the journey. What they never discuss is the fact that they still haven't decided where they want to go.

When we lose sight of these three characteristics of money— that it is symbolic, homogenizes, and is a means—we tend to get disoriented and begin gradually to believe that money is the key to the satisfaction of all needs. At that point money ceases to be a tool and becomes our master. It distracts our attention from those desires that money can't satisfy and directs it toward those that it does. For if we have money we tend to think of what it can buy—we forget about our own·needs and goals and become shoppers and catalog readers. There is a world of difference between saying "What do I want to do tonight?" and saying "What's at the movies?" In the first case we set our own goals; in the second we merely choose among options that someone else has offered us. Whenever we forget what money is, it seduces us into abandoning our own goals and settling for a multiple-choice test designed by someone else. We may still choose, but the range of possibilities often has no relevance to our deepest needs.

When people rebel against money they say that the best things in life are free—things like bodily pleasures—especially sex—love, friendship, beauty, adventure, fresh air and pleasing surroundings, health, psychological well-being, self-esteem, spiritual development, inner joy. These things are hard to homogenize. Yet our economy has come to depend on getting people to believe that there is nothing in life money can't buy. This is a basic tenet of Moneythink, since money is *designed* to reduce all things to a single homogeneous scale. Hence those who are its most devoted servants are continually engaged in an effort to enlarge money's sphere of influence—to make more and more satisfactions marketable. As a nation we mount a continual assault on those parts of life that cannot be bought. The advertising industry, for example, has never tried to hide its effort to convince the public that every human need can be satisfied by buying something. You get health by buying drugs, doctors, breakfast foods and—when people begin to realize that "less is more"—diet books, diet foods, jogging equipment, exercycles, and so on. You get love and friendship by buying perfume, aftershave lotion, cosmetics, deodorants, toothpaste, mouthwash, wine, beer, and cola. You get beauty and adventure by buying a package tour to the Orient.

Even nature is a target. More and more of us are having to pay for fresh air and a tolerable environment. We are even trained to believe that camping in the woods—"getting away from it all"—is possible only if we buy a lot of "it all" and take it with us in the form of expensive camping equipment. To breathe really clean air on land for more than a day at a time thus requires an initial investment of several hundred dollars, not counting the car that gets you back to nature in the first place and helps destroy it as you enjoy it.

One reason why so many advertisements imply that sexual delights will accompany purchase of their products is that sexual pleasure has nothing whatever to do with money and hence challenges its supremacy. Whole industries are devoted to trying to make sexual attractiveness something that can be purchased in a store. This is why, for example, Americans are so obsessed with deodorants. People are sexually attracted by some odors, repelled by others. The goal of the cosmetic industry is to deemphasize the attractive odors and get people to substitute commercial scents, after first persuading them that their own natural odors are repugnant. This is one way of tying sex into the economy—of making people feel they need money to obtain sexual gratification, so that social status and sexual success can be homogenized. It has had the unfortunate by-product of creating a whole nation of people filled with the kind of obsessive, self-conscious self-dissatisfaction that we usually associate with the onset of puberty and acute cases of acne.

Money was meant to be our servant. But when we depend on servants too much they gradually become our masters, because we have surrendered to them our ability to run our own lives. This servant has grown so powerful it has convinced us that we are empty and must find ways to fill ourselves up—that we are full of holes and must continually plug our lacks and deficiencies with substances from outside. This feeling of emptiness or incompleteness—this desperate dependence on external substances without which we feel incomplete—is the very essence and nature of addiction, and addiction is what this book is all about. It deals with a very old, very simple, but very important question about money: do you rule money or does money rule you?

2

The Money on Your Back

[In a shipwreck] one of the passengers fastened a belt
about him with two hundred pounds of gold in it,
with which he was afterwards found at the bottom.
Now, as he was sinking—had he the gold?
Or had the gold him?

RUSKIN

In the city where I live there is a peasant neighborhood called Pasatiempo. The name conjures up images of dreamy Mexican villages with peasants sleeping the noon away, but there are no peasants in Pasatiempo. High above the city on a charming hillside, gathered comfortably around a golf course, Pasatiempo is where the rich live.

The Bicentennial Year brought a severe drought to the city, and restrictions on water use were imposed. We were asked not to wash our cars with hoses or water our gardens more than every other day, and various water-saving gadgets were distributed. Even before emergency restrictions were imposed, city water usage was down almost 20 percent in response to requests for restraint in using water. In the entire city, only Pasatiempo failed to respond. Instead, they *increased* their consumption by 50 percent.

This little event set me thinking about wealthy people and our attitudes toward them, for it held what were to me two

16

mysteries. The first mystery was the behavior of the Pasatiem-pans themselves: what drove them to engage in this feverish consumption? It was as if at the very first mention of a shortage they all ran out and turned their hoses on, which doesn't quite fit our Hollywood stereotype of the wealthy householder as sedate, imperturbable, and faintly British. We might expect them to ignore the water shortage, but our cultural program-ming doesn't prepare us to see them aggravating it.

The second mystery is that there was no outcry when word of this abuse became public. We might have expected that the news would sap the desire of other residents to conserve water—that such a severe break in the ranks would have led to a demoralized retreat. Instead, water conservation was so suc-cessful that all mandatory restrictions were removed. It almost seemed as if people *expected* the rich to take more than their share—as if it were their prerogative. The poor suddenly ap-peared to me as tolerant parents indulging a greedy child, recognizing his inability to control his impulses.

As I thought about this I began to feel that all our contradic-tory and confusing ideas about wealth were missing something important. The capitalist view, for example—still widely ac-cepted among the general public—is that wealth is nature's reward for special cleverness, industry, or talent. Rich men are widely assumed to have some kind of ability or competence, despite the fact that in most cases their wealth was inherited.

The Marxist view sees wealth largely in social terms. It stresses the corrupting influence of money, but it pays little attention to the fact that some people are more susceptible to this infection than others. The Marxist theory of wealth addic-tion is a lot like the American theory of drug addiction, which would have us believe that if the evil pusher can just manage to sneak a little heroin into any unsuspecting victim he can count on adding a lifelong addict to his string of customers.

The early days of psychoanalysis saw some promising begin-nings toward a psychology of money. Freud and his disciples talked about the preoccupation with money displayed by the "anal personality," one who was always hoarding and accumulating and tidying things up; rectal itching was discovered to be a common nervous symptom of the wealthy. But this interest in the neurotic side of wealth began to wane as the psychoanalysts themselves became wealthy, and in recent decades they have tended to concentrate more on the anality of poverty and untidiness.

Money is certainly an addiction, and one to which few of us are altogether immune. But saying this—viewing the source of an addiction as a universal menace from which no one is safe—never seems to help. Facing the fact that some people are more prone to addiction than others may lull a few people into a false sense of security, but it seems to be a necessary step toward getting a handle on what it is inside us that responds to the bait. If a man thinks that cigarette addiction will be upon him when he smokes his first butt, he need never take a look at himself from the moment that threshold has been crossed. Self-understanding often begins, paradoxically, with looking smugly and analytically at the "poor unfortunate" in whom the addictive pattern is writ so large that we can see it clearly. Once the pattern has been dramatized in this way we can begin to detect it within ourselves.

I doubt that we Americans can come to terms with our own money neuroses without understanding the more florid pathology of the very rich, for it is our envy and admiration of the rich that supports their habit and keeps us hooked ourselves. American ideas about wealth are virtually unchanged since 1900, although intellectuals have advanced and countered such a variety of different arguments on the topic that they have now come full circle and imagine themselves to have disposed of the issue.

A recent man-in-the-street interview asked the passersby if they resented people with great wealth. All of them answered in the negative, arguing either that the wealthy had earned their wealth or that it was stupid to be resentful of a club one hoped one day to enter. If I am to enjoy the fantasy of being rich myself, in other words, I need to be convinced that the rich are somehow deserving.

It's easy to dismiss such attitudes as naive and foolish, but they seem to be what most ordinary people believe, and therefore they need to be taken seriously. What ordinary people *think,* furthermore, is very often the same as what intellectuals *act* on, whatever their ideological convictions, since intellectuals tend to suffer from a lack of communication between the head and the heart. Hence I would like to repeat some facts that are well known in the intellectual sense, but unknown in the sense that people have not yet begun to live as if they were true.

C. Wright Mills, the sociologist, showed some time ago that great wealth is not earned, but acquired. The extremely wealthy, in most cases, have simply inherited comfortable fortunes and used their position to multiply them grotesquely through investment. Of the 90 richest men in 1950, 68 percent came from wealthy families. Nor is it easy to make a case that the newly rich are any more deserving. They have certainly had a sharp eye for profit: those who didn't already own land on which oil was discovered apparently had the wit to acquire it. But, as we shall see in Chapter 4, this can be deceptive: a gambler always looks clever when he wins, but if ten men buy plots of land speculatively and oil is found on only one, that man is not necessarily more intelligent than the others. He may, of course, be more unscrupulous, and gain access, through bribery or other means, to information not available to his competitors. And, in fact, it is extremely rare to find a large fortune that wasn't founded in part on illegal or at least unethical practices.

In saying this I don't mean to be cynical. Great fortunes can almost never be acquired ethically for a very simple reason: *money is an instrument of trade and in an ethical trade everyone would come out at the end relatively equal.* If, then, at the end of a lifetime of exchange, one man comes out rich and the other poor, the poor man has been cheated and the rich man is a cheat. This is made explicit in the first rule of success in business: "buy cheap and sell dear," or, in other words, "cheat those with whom you deal." If our entire economic system is based on the exhortation to cheat, we can hardly be surprised or indignant to find that the biggest rewards go to those who are the biggest cheaters. The real question we need to ask ourselves is this: are these the people we want to reward?

Every society tries in some way to encourage those people whose skills or arts or personality traits are most valuable to it. We reward greed and sharp dealing and punish generosity and modesty. Perhaps this is what we want, but we ought to be a little more conscious of what we're doing and what price we're paying. A man trades with us all his life and ends up rich. Has he given us anything in exchange?

In most cases the answer is no. People get rich because they feel deprived and they don't ever *want* to give anything in return. If they wanted to give something in return, they obviously wouldn't be rich, since people get rich by buying cheap and selling dear—in other words, by taking much more than they give back.

Apologists for the rich have come up with many ingenious ways of avoiding this simple truth. They point to the philanthropic activities of the rich, the advantages of concentrating wealth in one spot, and the need to reward those who take special risks with their money. But to steal five hundred million and give back one is not what is meant by the word "charity." Furthermore, as we'll see when we examine the lives of the very wealthy in Chapter 4, many of the biggest moneymakers have given little or nothing to charitable causes.

If we didn't devote so much of our energy as a nation to making a few people very rich, we wouldn't need their donations. We funnel energy (and money) *away* from things we need so we can enrich a few (hoping, of course, that we'll be one of those lucky few). Then we try to beg some of it back to take care of necessities and feel grateful if we get a few scraps. This seems like a cumbersome way to reap the benefits of concentrated wealth. There are many others: taxes, union dues, retirement funds, collections of all kinds. Within our own society we have repeatedly demonstrated that there are better ways to concentrate money. And as to risk—people will risk in a great cause as well as in a selfish one. Furthermore, the corporation came into being as a way of spreading risk, so there is no particular reason why great fortunes need be essential to the process.

Our society is run like a great lottery: everyone pays so a few can win. An attempt is then made to meet the needs of the society and its people as a by-product of this process. Just as state lotteries take a percentage of the income to help balance their budgets and to run the lottery itself (including running advertisements encouraging people to *participate* in the lottery!)—so as a nation we run a gigantic and highly corrupted lottery, using some income to pay prizes (making certain people rich), some to take care of business (feeding and clothing the people, supporting science, the arts, education, defense), and some to advertise (telling ourselves repeatedly how wonderful this system is). Yet many of the same people who feel strongly that state lotteries are a foolish way to generate funds for a state budget think our economic system is perfectly rational.

Apologists for our system claim that making a few people rich in this way brings benefits for everyone. People work hard to get rich and the rich spend their money and keep everything moving. This is the well-known "trickle-down" theory. The name itself is refutation enough: we don't call it the "pour-down" theory. The basic problem with the whole idea is that the rich *don't* spend in proportion to their wealth. That's why they are rich. They take more than they give and they save more than they spend and they buy cheap and sell dear. This is why money coming from the rich to the poor only trickles.

On the other hand, when we arrange to direct money to the poor it bounces right back up to the rich again, since the poor *do* spend. They *have* to, to survive. Furthermore, the rich have so arranged things that the poor usually have to buy dear and sell cheap, so that what is slow to come down is quick to go up. Although the "trickle-down" theory is so specious on the face of it that it hardly merits a rebuttal, it is one of the official beliefs of our society, and I'll discuss it in more detail in Chapter 6.

I have argued that our economic system is a kind of lottery that rewards the few at the expense of the many. This is not to say that those who become rich are merely lucky. As we shall see in Chapter 4, they are, as a group, extremely well focused on the narrow goal of making money and develop refined skills in achieving that goal. They know what they want and they go after it, and as a nation we value that kind of concentration and initiative. And rightly so—concentration and initiative are wonderful traits. But one can exercise these capacities in ways that have nothing to do with money. There are many opportunities to do wonderful things in our world—opportunities that are rarely seized because people are so distracted by money.

Not all the newly rich get something for nothing. Every once in a while a fortune may be built on a contribution of some kind. An artist or entertainer, for example, provides pleasure to people in return for the money he or she earns. An invention may prove popular. But it usually takes an organization of some kind to make someone a millionaire. An invention, for example, must be manufactured, promoted, distributed. Industrial empires don't just emerge, and they aren't built by a single hand. Every millionaire has a coterie of loyal partners and devoted followers, for many different skills are needed. Yet of all these diverse and vital talents only one or two individuals reap the monetary rewards. It seems to be a case of "to each according to his need." Some participants in a successful enterprise are content with a comfortable salary and the satisfaction of doing their jobs well and being recognized for it. Others are more needy, more insecure. They feel compelled to take more than their share because their addiction is always competitive: what they have is not satisfying if others have it, too. Taking seems to be gratifying for them only if it involves taking *away* from others.

This is the only way we can make sense of the frequency with which wealthy people hoard or overconsume during a shortage. When things are scarce, in other words (as in wartime), many rich people not only take more than their share, as they do at all times, but also take *more than usual.* In the energy crisis of 1973–74, for example, wealthy people purchased large, expensive, fuel-devouring cars by the thousands, apparently just to show that they could afford them. Things have value for true wealth addicts only in proportion to how much *other* people want or need them.

In my city there is a yacht harbor with hundreds of expensive boats. On the finest day of the year far less than a quarter are in use and for most of the year all but a handful sit idle, to be used once a month or even once a year. Most of them seem to be there, behind the locked fence, as a symbol to be admired and envied. They exist, in other words, to create wealth addiction in others. If so, then all wealth addicts are pushers by definition, because *wealth is the only form of addiction in which the addict gets high off other people's withdrawal symptoms.*

Many people dream of owning their own boat and more are doing it every day, but as an investment it ranks a little below playing the slot machines. To own and moor a boat in a populated area costs so much that one would have to use it at least three times a week every week of the year to make it cheaper than renting one by the day. If all these boats were made available for rental to the public the rental rates would be driven down and usage would greatly increase, but even then many of the boats would probably lie idle. Certainly there would be enough boats for those who could afford it to sail by the day as often as they wanted or were able. The real function of owning such a boat seems to be to prevent other people from enjoying it.

Boats are not unique in this respect. Airports housing private planes find few in use at any given time. And in my city the choicest shorefront homes with the most magnificent views sit empty most of the year with shades drawn over their windows, preventing poorer people from enjoying the beauty they command.

The most extreme example is art theft. When we hear that some masterpiece has been stolen from a museum we think of burglars with tools, masks, and other low-life accoutrements. Surprisingly little attention is devoted to the fact that behind every major art theft there has to be a millionaire, for no one else can afford to buy the stolen goods. Great art can't be "fenced" in the ordinary way. It can be purchased only by a wealthy collector who hides it away for personal satisfaction.

When I first voiced this idea I was told that it was a weak example, bordering on the absurd, and when a Rembrandt was later stolen from a museum in San Francisco, the museum's curator of paintings expressed the same skepticism. He scoffed at the idea of "some unscrupulous, cognac-sipping connoisseur buying the Rembrandt to keep it in a vault, just to take it out at midnight—that's Hollywood stuff." He was trying to make the case that the painting would be returned soon—too famous to be marketable. His optimism was not shared, however, by a man in the best position to know—the president of the International Association of Art Security, Alan Baer, who predicted it would be sold in international black markets. Baer pointed out that Interpol keeps a list of most-wanted stolen masterpieces, including works by Rubens, Bellini, Correggio, and Toulouse-Lautrec, that have not been recovered: "Their fame didn't help." Art theft, he said, is a big business, amounting to over $50 million a year. "There are rich and unscrupulous collectors all over the world."

Nothing could reveal more clearly what wealth addiction is

all about. A rich man pays a thief to steal a painting from a museum, where it can be enjoyed by millions of people (including the rich man) and bring it to him so he can possess it exclusively. Perhaps he can't even enjoy it very fully, since it must be kept in a place where it won't be discovered. The real satisfaction for the collector is the *exclusiveness* of the possession—the fact that poorer people are deprived of the pleasure of seeing it.

I use the term "wealth addiction" to describe the psychological condition of rich people. Many readers will find this language objectionable. Surely, they will argue, not all wealthy people are addicts. Addiction implies something feverish and grasping—utterly out of keeping with the quiet good breeding of the securely wealthy who sit on the boards of charitable institutions and universities.

But alas, quantity is crucial in all addictions—we rely heavily on it to tell the addict from the nonaddict. We don't call a man who takes heroin once or twice a year an addict, nor do we call a woman who drinks once a week an alcoholic. We have begun to acknowledge, however, that anyone who consumes more than a half-pint of hard liquor every day *is* an alcoholic, whether he or she knows it or not. By the same token I think we can reasonably maintain that anyone with assets of more than $1 million or a net income of over $50,000 a year is a wealth addict. This is not to say, of course, that they are the *only* addicts. There are millions of poor people who are potential wealth addicts, just as there are many potential alcoholics who have never taken a drink. But it's a mistake to view all poor people as closet wealth addicts just as it's a mistake to view all teetotalers as potential alcoholics. There are many, many people who are genuinely indifferent to money, just as there are many who are indifferent to alcohol. The idea that everybody wants money is propaganda circulated by wealth addicts to make themselves feel better about their addiction. Other addicts do the same thing. Alcoholics surround themselves with heavy drinkers and are able to imagine that drunks are the only people who ever have any fun, since they are the only people they ever *see* having fun. Wealth addicts have an easier time of it than other addicts since they exercise a lot of influence in our society, particularly through the media. Yet despite this fact more and more people in our society are kicking the habit, as we'll see in Chapter 7.

Now, it might be objected that some people are just born with money, or keep it out of habit, or are just getting paid well for what they do, or just need security, and so on. The same kinds of arguments are used by alcoholics: they come from a hard-drinking family, they just drink socially or when they need a lift, or because having cocktails is just a pleasant habit. "Just a habit" is a particularly odd excuse since having a habit is what we're talking about.

Quantity and consistency are irrefutable symptoms of addiction—lack of addiction can be proven only by the ability *painlessly* to go without. It is quite true that merely having a lot of money is not in itself a sign of addiction. The wealth addict *maintains* a high income or *increases* it. A nonaddict might drift into wealth from time to time but would not cling to it, or seek more. One proves a lack of addiction by letting go.

A more serious argument is that wealth (like alcohol, tobacco, caffeine, marijuana, sugar, Valium, or cocaine) simply makes people happy and should not be considered necessarily addictive, even in large quantities. There are certainly people who have had great wealth, enjoyed it, and lost it. These people are not addicts. But I don't know of anyone who has had it, clung to it, and not eventually become addicted.

The secret strategy of all addicts is to represent their addiction as a benign human frailty to which everyone is more or less subject. To the tobacco addict, everyone smokes except a few health nuts; to the alcoholic, everyone drinks except a few puritans. The Don Juan who uses sex compulsively to bolster his sagging ego paints himself as just especially virile or lusty. And the wealth addict argues that everyone is after money except a few deranged hermits—that he is merely more aggressive and competent in his quest.

What distinguishes wealth addicts from other addicts is that they have been largely successful in selling this delusion to the general public. Tobacco addicts are fighting a rear-guard action against the nonaddicted population. Alcoholics are increasingly recognized as such. And both men and women are getting better and better at telling the difference between true erotic passion and a desperate ego. But as the psychiatrist Edmund Bergler points out, "The neurotic approach to money has the approval and social backing of the wealthy segment of our society and is therefore under no external pressure. There are very few wealthy people with a normal approach to money." Wealth addicts have the propaganda machinery of the entire society at their disposal, working full-time to perpetuate their self-deceptions. As a result, the neurotic defense mechanisms of the most extreme addicts have become the official ideology of our society: greed, duplicity, ruthlessness, self-centeredness, and a kind of narrowness—the ability to focus and concentrate on a limited goal to the exclusion of all else—are apparently the traits our society wants to reward.

There is no question in my mind that a narrow and ruthless concentration on money tends to bring the "success" that wealth addicts seek, but in the long run it also breeds dissatisfaction and discontent. It isn't easy, of course, to prove that one person is happier or unhappier than another. I'm sure most people could think of some rich person somewhere who seems happier than the general run of human beings. There are certainly alcoholics who seem cheerful, too, as well as merry smokers and serene-looking junkies. But it's one thing to say that some people seem buoyant even in the throes of an addiction, and quite another to say that the addiction itself makes them happy. Some people are happy in the throes of a mortal illness, too, but I never heard anyone argue that cancer makes people happy and we should all try it. I have known some drunks who were happy at times, but I've known no one who devoted a long life to alcohol and didn't suffer from it, and I believe the same to be true of wealth, as I'll try to show in Chapter 4.

One of the main reasons wealth makes people unhappy is that it gives them too much control over what they experience. They try to translate their own fantasies into reality instead of tasting what reality itself has to offer. This is usually an enervating and disappointing pastime. When you can control what comes to you in life, life itself loses most of its excitement. Almost nothing is unexpected since wealth tends to protect you from the unexpected. Your world gets filled up with the products of your own mind, and this deprives you of true novelty. A motel chain used to advertise that, in traveling, "the best surprise is no surprise." One wonders why people bother to leave home if they are trying to avoid surprises. For myself and other travelers I've talked with, the unexpected adventures, surprises, and crises of travel have produced the most wonderful experiences. They have also provided some painful ones, but if you don't allow for the possibility of pain, you cut off the possibility of pleasure. I can't escape the strong impression that whenever a traveler "rolls with" the adventure and lets it take him or her where it will, the outcome is usually enjoyable: kindly strangers or a sense of humor turn misery into joy—wrecked plans open doors into worlds previously unknown. This is what travel is all about—adventure. If you risk nothing, you get nothing. Yet whether in travel or in everyday life, wealth serves to eliminate adventure and challenge, smooth over rough spots, tame the unexpected, and bury novelty. The "successful" individual, after all, is bent on trying to seize destiny and control it. (If you roll with the adventure you may not keep your riches very long.) The wealthy tend to respond to frustrations and adventures with intense irritability. The fact that their will is being thwarted is usually of more concern to them than the fact that a door is being opened. Nonaddicts are people who would rather live a full life than maintain control. That's why they are seldom rich for long.

When you can control your world enough to stay permanently wealthy, you're likely to find yourself starved for challenge. Throughout the ages the securely wealthy have suffered from boredom and have tried desperately to overcome it by *purchasing* novelty in the form of diversions and entertainments. This is self-defeating in the long run, for true novelty, by definition, can't be controlled. It's pretty rare to be intensely surprised by something you've bought. Since nothing is risked in these endeavors, eventually they become boring, and you are tempted to raise the ante. How long can you enjoy a game in which nothing is at stake? How exciting is a fox hunt, or a catered safari with all the comforts of home? What kind of adventure is it when all possible dangers have been anticipated and ensured against (and if anything unexpected happens, someone gets fired)? So there must be new diversions, new pleasures, new artists, new clowns, and often an element of violence tends to creep in. The amusements become cruel, as in Rome, or dangerous: fast horses, fast cars, fast boats.

But this isn't all. The heart needs to find out if love can be won without any control or manipulation or power or money. Am I lovable for myself? naked of all those things that attract and compel others? The mind shuns this test and tries to load the dice on every throw. In love, the rich or successful man or woman feeds on empty emotional calories. I become a success so that people will love me, but after I have become a success, can I believe in what I get? If you gain fame, power, or wealth, you won't have any trouble finding lovers—but they will be people who love fame, power, or wealth. If you go fishing with worms, you will catch whatever eats worms. But love isn't fishing. What we want most of all is to be loved for who we are, without bait. The more bait, the more doubt:

> *If I were a carpenter,*
> *And you were a lady,*
> *Would you marry me anyway?*
> *Would you have my baby?*

Finally, wealth makes it very difficult to learn from life, and grow. With so much control, so much insurance, so much power to materialize your daydreams, you tend to lose your sensitivity to reality. There's a beautiful subtlety to our relationship with nature and necessity, a fine reciprocity: we play with necessity, it teaches us. We discover its edges, its soft places. We learn when and why it opens to us and brings us delight. When it closes and frowns. We learn capacities and depths in ourselves we never knew we had. We learn joys in the world we never knew existed.

The human Ego is a narrow thing. It knows only the past. It keeps trying to do today what worked yesterday. It tends to be rigid and limited—to wear blinders so it will see only what's straight ahead. It is always worrying about safety—that's its job. It has very little imagination. It is too *busy* to have any imagination, so we make a terrible mistake when we give it too much power.

Wealth tends to do just that—give the Ego too much power. You begin to feel that the obstacles and frustrations of life are not signposts to be learned from, but meaningless nuisances, not to be borne. You acquire a bulldozer mentality: instead of entering into a mutual relationship with life you simply charge down a single track until you run yourself into the ground. Learning and growth are very difficult with wealth because they depend on experiences in real life, and wealth enables one to buy *out* of life. It provides the wherewithal to cling to every outworn fantasy, pathway, or goal—to grasp every out-grown security blanket more tightly—to control your input in such a way that you never need to change or develop.

Rubber wheels and shock absorbers have so disconnected us from the land that we no longer know how to relate to it except as an obstacle to be smoothed or cut down or paved over, and this has made us insensitive and our world ugly. We know how to build the shortest or cheapest way any-where, but not the prettiest, or most thrilling, or most sub-tle, or most invigorating, or most elegant. Wealth produces the same kind of sterile and unresponsive environment on the personal level. You can never find out, for example, what your most satisfying calling might be, since experience need play so little part in its evolution. If you want to be a writer, you can pay a vanity press to publish your book. If you fancy yourself as an opera singer, you can hire a hall, as one wealthy woman used to do periodically, and hire the audience to go with it. Only the hardest reality can force many people to recognize a lack of talent and shift to greener pastures. Whatever *real* talents lie dormant in a wealth addict may never be discovered, because his or her most juvenile self-images can be acted out indefinitely.

When we have too much conscious power to shape our own destiny our future is constricted by our own narrow goals—our desire to make the world safe for ourselves. Safety is stagnation, for only when we're risking something does life become worth living. Wealth itself is one kind of security, and its possession makes possible many other kinds. Vitality and growth can be regained only if the wealth itself is risked.

But poverty also makes people miserable. Growth and hap-piness depend on some ability to choose among options, and the truly poor are unable to enjoy this luxury. While the wealthy are stifled by having too much control over their lives, the poor are stifled by having too little. As I shall show in

Chapter 6, the poor are oppressed by necessity not only because wealth addicts have hogged all the resources, but also because addicts have arranged things so that it is difficult to survive in our society without *becoming* a wealth addict.

3

The Four Signs of Addiction

*The opportunities of living are diminished
in proportion as what are called the "means"
are increased.*
THOREAU

Wanting money is not in itself a sign of addiction. The man or woman who dreams occasionally of having a lot of money to travel, buy clothes, own a yacht, give huge parties, and buy presents for friends and relatives is not necessarily an addict. Even saving money is not automatically a sign of addiction, nor is working hard to earn some. The man who works hard earning money in order to buy a house he wants is not an addict. An addict buys a house he *doesn't* want in order to make money through speculation.

Wealth addiction is more than having money or saving money or dreaming of money. Wealth addiction has to do with our *attitude* toward money. Hence it can easily hide itself behind some harmless desire. How do we tell if we're addicted? If we look at the average middle-class American, and the more comfortable, secure members of the working class, who have enough to eat and a viable home and car, how many of them are Closet Addicts—awaiting only the opportunity to give themselves over completely to that most ferocious of all addic-

33

tions? At what point does a natural desire to eat well, be comfortable, and have pleasant surroundings slip over into disease? How do we detect signs of addiction in ourselves?

It's easy to confuse an addiction with a simple need. We all have needs for food, water, sex, warmth, love, and so on. We may also feel the need at times for entertainment, solitude, an ego boost, a walk in the country—almost anything can occasionally be the object of need. And any need can also become an addiction. An addiction is a need that is not only (1) intense and (2) chronic, but also (3) feels as if it were essential to our sense of wholeness. Addictions have to do with our feelings about ourselves: if you think you would feel incomplete, less of a person, or unable to function well without something—even for a little while—then you are addicted to that something. An addiction is something you use to fill what seems to be a lack in yourself.

We all need food, for example, but if you can't imagine yourself being able to go on a fast, then you're addicted to food. We all need love and sexual gratification, but if you simply can't imagine yourself spending several months without a sexual partner, then you're addicted to sex, using it to prop up your Ego in some way. It has little to do with how much appetite you have—gastronomical or sexual—or how much discomfort a fast, or several months alone at sea or in the woods, might cause you. It has to do with whether or not you *think* that this discomfort would overwhelm your psyche. The fear that the deprivation would be overwhelming is what distinguishes need from addiction.

Glenn Turner, the multimillionaire, was once quoted as saying: "Without money I'm nothing." It would be hard to find a simpler statement of what wealth addiction is about. When you feel you need money to complete your personality or public image, then it is appropriate to speak of addiction.

Wealth addiction takes several forms. Some people are primarily *Money Addicts.* They make it, accumulate it, and never want to do anything with it. Others are *Possession Addicts.* When they achieve wealth they like to give it concrete expression in the form of houses, clothes, cars, yachts, and so on. Still others are primarily *Power Addicts.* The minute they acquire some money they want to use it to gain political power or simply to bully those around them. Then there are *Fame Addicts,* who want to make their mark in society, to be seen, noticed, accepted by the "in crowd," or, as a last resort, memorialized for posterity; and they use money to this end. Finally there are simple *Spending Addicts,* who aren't necessarily interested in possessions but like to have "money to burn" in their pockets—to travel, entertain, amuse themselves. This last category is my own special weakness.

Now it may seem odd to call all these people wealth addicts, but as long as it's money that's being accumulated and held on to, no other term will do. Money, as we've already observed, can stand for anything. Some people who are addicted to fame or power never accumulate any money to speak of. Others disclaim any interest in money, yet somehow end up with hundreds of millions. The former are not wealth addicts, the latter are, by definition. It doesn't matter what the money *stands* for, any more than it matters what alcohol or heroin stands for.

Bunker Hunt, for example (who, like his father before him, was at one time billed as the richest man in America), was quoted as saying that his only real goal in life was to make a profit, "because that's how you judge success or failure in life. . . . Money never really meant anything to me. . . . My father never really cared about money, either. It was just sort of how they kept the score." Yet money is by no means the only way to "keep score" in life. Like many billionaires, H. L. Hunt was unostentatious and lived simply—the same was true of Henry Ford. Yet somehow each of these men managed to accumulate over a billion dollars. If money was of no interest to them, why did they amass so much of it? Why didn't they give it away? Who keeps old scorecards? H. L. Hunt may have lived simply, but he was also notorious in refusing to give the money he didn't care for to charitable causes. When wealth addicts say they're not interested in money, what they usually mean is that they're not interested in *spending* it.

There are four major signs of wealth addiction:

1. A closing hand.
2. Confusion about goals.
3. Increasing possession, decreasing use.
4. Tension and search behavior.

THE CLOSING HAND

A key sign of any addiction is the fear that we would be unable to face life without some form of external security—a drink, a fix, proper clothing, a sexual partner, a full wallet. It's the feeling that naked and alone we would be incomplete. The symptoms of addiction are grasping, controlling, clinging, ensuring. Addiction is a closed fist, the conviction that if we let go of what we have today it won't come back tomorrow. In my own life I've been addicted to many things, and the way I learned to detect addiction was very simple: the things I was addicted to I rarely let myself run out of. (Other people are less compulsive, but feel it is a calamity when they *do* run out.)

Addicts stockpile both material and intangible satisfactions, and we are all addicts to some degree. We may stockpile food, liquor, money, fuel. We may also stockpile good deeds ("Brownie points"), potential lovers, social contacts, potential adventures, free time, and so on. There is nothing, tangible or spiritual, that can't be stockpiled.

When I was a cigarette smoker I usually had several days' supply around and became very uneasy if I got down to a pack or two. I have gone through the same process with imported wines and special coffees. Yet very few of my favorite foods have ever aroused this obsessive concern.

There is a world of difference between feeling that a certain kind of experience would make the day bright and feeling that the day will be spoiled without that experience. An addict always sees the glass as half empty rather than half full. He tries to make sure that the things he *knows* he wants or needs are available. In the process he often cuts himself off from other sources of satisfaction that he is *unaware* of needing or wanting. This lack, in fact, feeds the addiction, for the addict will be aware of deprivation, even if he is mistaken about its cause.

Imagine that a man lives in the wilderness in a region where there are two springs. In one spring the water contains a great deal of iron, but no other minerals. In the second can be found zinc and a variety of other trace elements essential to human survival. The man is very aware of the iron in the first spring. He can taste it and has conceived a firm belief that the iron is good for him and gives him strength. He starts to worry about whether the spring will survive the visits of animals and decides to live near it to protect it. Needless to say, he never goes near the other spring, and after some time his body begins to feel the lack of the elements it contains. Blinded by his addiction (or conviction—they are much the same thing) he believes that his weakness and disagreeable symptoms are a result of not getting enough of his iron-filled water. He starts drinking twice as much as before and now begins to experience symptoms from excess of iron. And so on.

In most kinds of addiction the harm comes not from the substance itself but from the fact that the addiction distracts us from other things we need—substances that nourish, experiences that feed and support and gratify us. This deprivation in turn reinforces the addiction.

Similarly, with wealth addiction, the harm lies less in wanting money or security than with the fact that our concern with these things deprives us of more nourishing human satisfactions—love, friendship, adventure, physical well-being, and so on. Furthermore, our pursuit of money and security not only deprives us but tends to deprive our neighbors as well, thus increasing the general feeling of scarcity in our environment.

CONFUSION ABOUT GOALS

Many years ago, when I used to do my own income tax, I often found myself spending absurd amounts of time on those ambiguous deductions that involved a certain amount of estimate making. I say absurd not only because it wasn't pleasurable time (to say the least) but also because it wasn't profitable even from a purely economic viewpoint: I would sometimes spend an hour playing with a deduction that saved me only a few dollars. The problem was that I wanted to maximize the deduction yet keep it reasonable enough so that I could avoid an audit, or at least defend it—a common problem, familiar to all income tax filers and blackjack players.

During those moments, as I tried different combinations—trying to balance the possible gain against the possible risk, as well as maintaining some minimal sense of personal integrity—I always experienced a mild feeling of disorientation, as if I had somehow lost my bearings. To say that I felt as if I were drowning in a sea of meaningless calculations is perhaps overstating things a bit, but it captures the flavor. I always ended by feeling tense and a little confused. Had I considered all the possibilities? Made the right choice? Certainly I made far too many calculations.

I have come to recognize that sensation as peculiar to certain kinds of encounters with money. Not all, certainly: I've had some very pleasant affairs with money, even if the most enjoyable ones were rather brief. The sense of disorientation occurs only when money takes over the helm and starts calling the shots—that is, when I forget what it is *I* want, and start thinking solely about how to save or accumulate money—

THE FOUR SIGNS OF ADDICTION □ 39

when money becomes an end in itself . . . when I become a slave to Moneythink.

This happens often in the daily lives of most Americans, but we have found ways of numbing ourselves to it, as we do with so many of the annoyances and abrasions of modern life. There have been times, for example, when I would go into a store and have trouble deciding whether to buy one expensive shirt I liked very much or two cheap ones I liked only moderately. The money would often derail me from the basic question of what I *wanted*. For while some people like having a quantity of clothes to choose from, I much prefer having a small number of things I really enjoy. For me these luxuries have even proved economical, since I wear them until they wear out, while my bargains sit in drawers until I give them away. But it doesn't really matter which way we choose—what matters is that the choice be based on our own desires rather than purely on considerations of maximizing wealth: on Moneythink.

But what of the poor, who can afford only one cheap shirt or none at all? If they don't think about maximizing money, they'll stay poor. Doesn't my statement really apply only to the affluent middle class, who have the luxury of choice?

The answer is no. When you're poor, being an addict might help you get rich, but it is far more likely to expose you to the possibility of being exploited by other addicts: most advertising, after all, is designed to appeal to the addictive side of our natures. Con men argue that you can't cheat an honest man— that the "mark" is usually a victim of his own greed. Whether this is true or not, many of the more notorious wealth addicts in our society achieved their positions by manipulating the success fantasies of their neighbors. Our economy is based on the exploitation of greed: if I can convince you that you're cheating me in our exchange, then I'll be able to cheat you.

Let's get back to the poor. Say I'm a poor man with only enough money in my pocket to buy a cheap shirt. I pass a store that has a sale on shirts. My choice is to buy a cheap shirt or to buy no shirt. The issue is still the same: is my choice determined by my own desire or by Moneythink? I may want to spend my last dime on a shirt. (I once knew a wealthy "self-made man" who in his youth had been out of a job in a strange town with only a few pennies in his pocket. Instead of spending them on food or a bed he had bought a useless ornament on impulse. Since his luck began to change soon afterward he always kept this ornament as a reminder of the lowest point in his fortunes.) On the other hand, I may want to save every penny in an effort to lever myself out of the vicious cycle of poverty. Both decisions are perfectly valid.

Moneythink has nothing to do with this. Moneythink is what the store owner tries to activate by having a sale. Moneythink says, "If you spend your money here, now, it will save you money in the long run." Moneythink argues that you must never lose a single opportunity to buy cheap or sell dear and hence accumulate money, regardless of how you feel about what you're buying or selling—whether you *want* it or not. Moneythink demands that you be devoted to the marketplace 24 hours a day, always on call, and that you be relatively indifferent to what it is that is being bought and sold.

A nonaddict may go into the store because she knows she wants a cheap shirt and thinks she might find one she likes there. An addict goes in because there's a sale, even though she doesn't know what she wants. The difference is subtle but vastly important, and it affects rich and poor alike. Rich or poor, if you're susceptible to Moneythink, you're open to exploitation by other addicts.

There is no halfway with Moneythink. If you want to accumulate a fortune, you have to concentrate on it every waking hour, to the exclusion of all else, because however dedicated *you* are, there are even more extreme addicts out there, and wealth addiction is a competitive game. As Joseph Thorndike, Jr., observes, the "most common characteristic of those who acquire great wealth is their dedication to that single goal."

Michael Phillips's "First Law of Money" is that "money will

come when you are doing the right thing." Like most of Phillips's observations, this depends largely on one's being educated and middle-class, but it contains an important truth. Money often tends to divide our energies: we alter and divert our efforts to make sure we have "enough" money. But money in the long run follows energy. If you divide your energy you will ultimately lose money. People have become rich either by being totally devoted to money or by completely ignoring it— becoming utterly absorbed in creating or performing or inventing, and achieving monetary success as a by-product of that absorption. (Poor people usually can't mobilize their energies along a single track like this because they have to devote so much energy to their survival—they don't have the leisure to ignore money. Usually the best they can do is to get rich enough to provide this opportunity for their children.) Phillips seems to be saying that if you can't put *all* your energy into money then put it all into something you *can* put it into. There is, of course, a certain risk in this: money follows energy, but it may not arrive in a single lifetime. Still, you will probably have a more satisfying time of it than you will trying to pursue money directly.

A half-baked addiction makes you the perfect target for more committed addicts. They can count on you to play their game and lose. When you engage in Moneythink you are likely to become someone's mark. The few successful gamblers in the world live off the addictions of the many undisciplined ones. The world of entrepreneurs is similarly composed—like all competitive worlds—of a few winners and a lot of losers.

We don't hear much about the losers. Or even the minor successes who get swallowed up and destroyed by the big winners. The problem with playing the addict game is that if you lose, you've wasted your life for nothing, since everything was invested in the game. If you don't play, you can enjoy some kind of life, whether rich or poor, but once you enter the game you lose that possibility. Once you submit to Moneythink you're contracting to be some wealth addict's supplier.

Severe addicts are supported in their habit by all of us to some extent, but most especially by mild addicts.

I've described submersion in Moneythink as a kind of mini-psychosis, in which we get out of touch with our own wishes and reactions and sensitivities and lose ourselves in calculations. Yet the *language* of Moneythink is the language of rationality. To want money in itself, without a clear and immediate idea of the uses to which you want to put it, is to be crazy, for money in and of itself is worthless. Yet people who are hopelessly lost in this state of confusion, disorientation, and loss of self are considered in our society to be peculiarly sane.

They achieve this air of normality by being fixated on security so fervently and compulsively that it acts for them as a kind of North Star, orienting every action. But to do this they have to want security so much that it obliterates all other desires, interests, reactions, pleasures, and so on, and few of us are that insecure. For most of us, Moneythink is a wave that occasionally splashes over us, knocks us over, and causes us momentarily to lose our sense of direction. But for severe addicts, Moneythink is a tidal wave that picks them up and completely takes them over. They behave as if they know where they're going because they've given themselves over completely to the wave, to go wherever *it* goes. They have surrendered their emotional life and abdicated all power to Moneythink—much as an old, elegant hotel is absorbed by a chain and homogenized. Those who allow themselves to become completely dominated by Moneythink will never lack a star to steer by, but it is no longer linked to their own human, biological needs.

When you are swept away by Moneythink you become that rarest of all fictions, "economic man," on which most of economics has traditionally been founded. Moneythink homogenizes because money homogenizes. That, as we have seen, is what money is for. When you are swept away by Moneythink, you tend to believe that everything *can* be homogenized in this way—that if you have more money, you have more of everything. This makes your choices very simple: you never have to choose between money and something else, because there *is* no something else. You only choose between more money and less money, which is an easy choice for a wealth addict. A machine could do it.

Obviously, there are few cases of people who have completely and perfectly abdicated the conduct of their lives to Moneythink. But those who have come closest have become the richest.

Normally, our many wishes and feelings create a kind of mosaic, in which each one bumps against another before it can go too far. Hunger and sexual desire extinguish themselves when gratified and give way to other needs that become more pressing as these recede, and they in turn give way to others, and so on in a continuous round of waxing and waning. All these desires and moods balance and limit one another, forming natural boundaries.

But in the kingdom of Moneythink, there *are* no natural boundaries. All of our varied and separate desires—the "checks and balances" of our internal republic—have been homogenized and pressed into the service of a despotic ruler who says, "All these desires will be fulfilled when you have enough money." But *how much is enough?* What is left to use as a limit? When we subordinate other desires to money we lose our ability to recognize "enough." Those goals and desires that are capable of satisfaction have been coopted by money, and the desire for money *has no natural limit.* Since it cannot in itself satisfy anything, we can *never* have enough. A number of rich men have acknowledged that they could satisfy all their material needs—and even whims—with a fraction of what they hold, yet are unable to stop trying to make more. Once money is given priority there is no longer any basis for deciding when and where to stop accumulating.

Let's take a trivial example. Suppose you decide to make a little money by buying a house in an area where there is a real estate boom and selling it later at a large profit. Your goal is simply to make money—you're not interested in the house as such. You go to a realtor, who shows you several houses. How do you decide which one to buy? Normally, you would have all sorts of spontaneous reactions to each house, as you imagined yourself living in it with your own furnishings and so on. But how do you go about buying something you don't want? You have to suppress all these irrelevant responses and try to figure out which house can be resold the quickest and at the biggest profit. If you haven't given yourself over wholly to Moneythink, you will be torn between the economic irrelevance of your own tastes and the emotional irrelevance of Moneythink. But let's suppose you pass this hurdle and buy a good prospect that means nothing to you. The house must be rented while you wait for the price to rise. How will you treat your tenants? Moneythink has a clear position: you charge the very highest rent that you can get away with, give nothing in return, and toss the tenants out the minute the opportunity arises to make a big profit by reselling. If you retain any feelings of community responsibility or even mere human decency, you'll find yourself increasingly confused. How exploitive is exploitive *enough?* How exploitive is *too* exploitive? When should you sell—that is, how much profit is *enough* profit? Once you've given yourself over completely to Moneythink these questions, of course, no longer arise. You exploit as much as you can get away with, and you sell when you believe the market has peaked—no sooner and no later.

When you commit yourself wholly and unreservedly to Moneythink, in other words, many conflicts and confusions dissolve (this is the basic message of the "how-to-be-a-success" books). But Moneythink can hardly be said to bring serenity. Soul-searching and indecision give way to fevered calculations and endless vigilance. Once your house is sold you immediately want to buy something to make an even bigger profit, and so on. In short, to give yourself over to Moneythink is to become a terminal wealth addict and never draw another easy breath.

Most people make some kind of uneasy compromise with Moneythink. Even the rich often find themselves perplexed by its one-dimensionality and blunder about confusedly trying to find alternative systems of value. This is a particular problem in American society, where—since wealth has never been strongly tied to aristocratic responsibilities and obligations—the freest possible rein is given to Moneythink. Thorndike comments that "if the American super-rich have sometimes presented a rather frivolous and irresponsible image to the world, it is perhaps because they have not known what to do with themselves."

INCREASING POSSESSION, DECREASING USE

We are so used to the idea of possession in our society that it isn't easy to get any perspective about it. Most Americans assume that it's "just human nature" to want to own things. Yet more than 90 percent of all the human beings who have ever lived have been hunter-gatherers, and for most such people mobility has been so important that possessions were shunned as a useless encumbrance. A few tools and weapons might have been in one person's possession, but the sense of "mine" and "yours" was very weak indeed. Private ownership of land is also a very recent concept. The original inhabitants of the United States thought it ludicrous to imagine that a person could "possess" a segment of the land, which so obviously belonged to all living things and therefore to no one in particular. Human beings lived off the land on this planet for millions of years before anyone was arrogant enough to claim ownership.

Ownership almost always begins with stealing. People who have worked the same land for countless generations are as likely to think that the land owns *them* as that they own the land. Ownership as we know it begins when someone steals the land: a conqueror comes through, takes the land and the farmers and gives them to his lieutenants to tax and exploit. In effect, then, ownership has to be established over the land *because* it has been stolen. The people who have a real right to the land through custom and usage—who have lived with it for centuries in some kind of mutual harmony—don't need to claim ownership. The issue never arises until someone usurps it. Legal land ownership usually means: "It was given or sold to me by a series of owners who got it from the original thief." A landowner is in effect an accessory after the fact and a receiver of stolen goods.

Yet clearly, there is no turning back. We cannot at this moment in history recapture easily the sense of interconnection that preindustrial and especially preagricultural peoples had. We are trained to think of ourselves as separate entities from birth, and hence to grasp. Children are taught to "share," but as an act of *noblesse oblige,* of concession. In less individualistic societies sharing is more automatic because the sense of separateness is so little developed. We subtly train our children from birth that they are private beings with ownership rights. Then we very crudely and publicly teach them to share. In less private societies brothers and sisters may share rooms, beds, clothes, possessions, and never think of what "belongs" to them. In our society it's possible to find siblings fighting over possessions even when three or four live in one room.

The desire to possess exclusively, in other words, is not a given, except in a society like ours. This is not to say we are unique. Landholding aristocrats and grasping peasants around the world are obviously susceptible to the urge. It's just more highly developed here than at any other time or place in history. Thus we need to make a particularly special effort to look at it with fresh eyes.

To own or possess is to monopolize the use of something permanently. Hence the need to possess betrays a degree of insecurity. Possession is a way of *ensuring access* to whatever it is we want to use or enjoy: we are so anxious that the object be there when we want it that we are willing to insist that it be there even when we *don't* want it. Thus we have food on our shelves when we're not hungry, clothes in our closets that we're not wearing, cars in our driveways that we aren't driving, and so on. The rationale is that when we *do* want to eat, dress, or drive, we won't have to waste time looking around for the food, clothing, or transportation. This time saving is questionable, as we shall see, but it expresses the sense of urgency that lies behind the compulsion to possess.

One way to put ownership in perspective is to imagine an alternative. Suppose, for example, that all cars were accessible to everyone. If you wanted to go somewhere, you would just hop in the nearest car and drive off. When you reached your destination you would leave the car and someone else would use it. Some coordinating system would be necessary to keep track of the cars, maintain them, and let people know where the nearest car was if one wasn't in sight—probably there would be some need for hired drivers to move vehicles into depleted areas. In any case we would need only about a third as many vehicles as we now have. (Under such a system, of course, automobiles would be built much more for transportation and much less as status symbols, sexual fetishes, and potency substitutes. A man who wanted to pump up his masculinity might have to look around for a long time to find the right kind of car.)

Most Americans would object to this system, although it is obviously more practical, less wasteful, and would create a more pleasant environment. People want their own cars, and this reveals the real function of ownership: *ownership is a way of preventing others from having access to the thing we want to use.* There is a basic insecurity behind ownership: we want something before anyone else can get it or before it becomes scarce. Ownership is a way of grasping and clinging to something we are afraid will be taken away from us.

Wealth addiction has been characterized as a disease, and a disease is usually regarded as a departure from some norm. How, then, can ownership, which is a way of life in our society, be a symptom of a disease? We can call the society as a whole diseased, if we want, but this doesn't help us discriminate between those who merely share a cultural distemper and those who are in the grip of an acute virulent sickness.

Such a distinction can be made by comparing possession and use: clearly, the less a possession is used, the more violent and uncontrollable the addiction. It's understandable to want to ensure access to something that is used every day. But what of things that are used only once a month or once a year?

Possessions have to be cared for and maintained—cleaned, repaired, protected, moved about, and so on. Each time you buy something, you acquire, in effect, a new boss: someone who requires work from you. An owner is simply a servant with as many masters as he or she has possessions. Now, to work for a boss who gives you a great deal in return is quite reasonable. But what can be said of someone who serves many masters who provide almost nothing in return?

The important question here is not how much we own but how we spend our time—whether we spend it in enjoyment, or in tending, protecting, coercing, maintaining, controlling, or searching out potential *sources* of enjoyment. In the latter case we are simply janitors to our own desires. What a waste of time if such janitorial services are provided for pleasure sources that are rarely or never used!

An affluent middle-class person clearly spends a good deal of time as an unpaid janitor, while a person wealthy enough to have servants becomes an unpaid Head Janitor. From a strictly rational viewpoint, owning is an extremely inefficient way to maximize pleasure. Unless there is an extraordinary difference in cost or quality, or almost constant use, it makes more sense to rent just about anything, and leave it up to the renter to provide the janitorial services: the searching, the protecting, the maintaining. The renter, after all, makes a living by providing those services.

The relationship of pleasure to money is complex. For example, money is subject to diminishing returns of pleasure.

Indeed, beyond some point, the larger the new sum, the *lower* the return in pleasure. I would suggest that for most people the pleasure peak for a money windfall is about 5 percent of one's current income: up to that point, the more money the more pleasure; but beyond that point, the more money the *less* pleasure. This is so because a larger sum usually tempts us to enlarge our scale of living in some way—to make a major acquisition of real or personal property, change our life-style, or begin involving ourselves in the management of investments so as to generate *more* money. At somewhere around 5 percent most people begin to recategorize their financial status and the money is put to work to achieve this change. The pleasure begins to be lost, and it will take an even larger windfall next time to produce any effect. As Neil Simon once remarked, "Money brings some happiness. But after a certain point it just brings more money." Money produces the most pleasure when it is small enough not to affect how we define ourselves financially—when we can "blow it" on a treat of some kind.

People tend to create a mosaic of satisfactions to match their own special pattern of needs. We all need love, struggle, companionship, solitude, adventure, tranquility, nature, culture, exercise, rest, and so on, in varying forms and amounts, and we tend more or less automatically to build environments that will periodically satisfy these needs. The arrangement shifts and alters with our own internal balances, but the basic mosaic is often quite stable. Some pieces of the mosaic are more visible to us and we take better care of these; others we may lose sight of and neglect. I have long been fully aware, for example, of my needs for touching, for physical movement, for love, for companionship. More recently I have become aware that if I have too little time by myself I will feel it almost as a physical pain. Still more recently I have begun to notice my need to be near the ocean every now and then—it's like a trace chemical: I don't need much but I become uncomfortable without any. I also feel out of sorts when my life is totally devoid of struggle and conflict, though it may take a long time before I notice the lack.

A balanced mosaic of satisfactions is very nourishing, and makes people energetic and cheerful. The trouble with addictions is that they blur and blunt our sensitivity to this complex mosaic—they lead to oversimplification. A mosaic that suits us well is hard to build and easy to tear down. We create it gradually, subtly, and unconsciously, through trial and error. My point about money windfalls is that below 5 percent they tend to be used to fill gaps in our life-mosaic. Larger windfalls, on the other hand, lead us to recategorize our financial status and upset the balance of our current mosaic. We then have to create a new mosaic, not necessarily more satisfying but infinitely more cluttered. We still have the same assortment of needs—we just need more money (or think we do) to satisfy them.

Money can also produce genuine relief of pain. For poor people this is one of the primary meanings that money has. One way of looking at money is to say that for poor people money tends to *increase* the options available, while for the affluent money tends to *decrease* the options available. This is the net effect of the janitorial services that you have to provide either for your money or for the things you purchase with it. The time you have to spend as a janitor more than counteracts the options opened up by the money itself.

This is true, of course, only so long as we're *attached* to the money or to the possessions. If we stand willing to lose all of it, at any moment, then money will always increase the options available to us, except insofar as the possession of the money distracts us from the innumerable options that don't involve money at all. The more money people get, the more prone to wealth addiction they are, because they begin to think increasingly of those pleasures money can buy and decreasingly of all others. This leads them to stockpile material goods—to buy more than they can use, which creates a vicious circle. As they become immersed in material possessions the janitorial services escalate. This shrinks the time available for pleasure, and in response to the growing shortage people stockpile *more* possessions so that they will be instantly available should the need arise. This creates more janitorial work, and so on. The closets of the affluent are filled with ski equipment, golf equipment, scuba gear, camping gear, cameras, water skis, and so on, as well as books on how to do all these things. They have beautiful second homes, but when you pass by they aren't in them, or if they are, most often they're puttering about looking after the unending maintenance and equipment problems that such possessions demand.

TENSION AND SEARCH BEHAVIOR

Another sure sign of addiction is restlessness, and this afflicts the poor as much as the rich. Consider morphine addiction, for example. You can get hooked on morphine in two ways: first, by having it around a lot and taking it frequently, observing that it feels good and using it, when you feel mediocre, to make yourself feel better; second, by being in terrible pain and observing that morphine relieves that pain. The latter is the way poor people become wealth addicts: they suffer excruciating pain from their poverty and associate money—not unreasonably—with relief from that driving and unending pain. But whatever the origin, devoting their lives to money tends to give people a restless, driven quality. They find it almost impossible to pause and consider the long-range implications of their actions. They are impatient with obstacles, delays, subtleties. They are the kind of people who build nuclear power plants *before* figuring out how to dispose of the atomic wastes.

We all have moments like this—roaring down a breakdown lane to bypass a traffic jam, thereby making it worse; brushing aside children because they distract us from some frenzied purpose; using our authority, or the power of the majority, to override objections to some program we think we want. This impatience, this pushiness, is a sure sign of addiction. The addict's feeling that there is an empty place *inside* that can be filled only from *outside* forces the addict to engage in constant search behavior—to be always on the lookout for the missing ingredient. This is especially apparent when the addictive element is not something that can be physically absorbed, like drugs or alcohol, but is essentially symbolic and psychological, like wealth, power, fame, virtue, or attractiveness. In these cases gratification is always incomplete. The body has its limits but your Ego may not. You can overdose on heroin or alcohol, but you cannot overdose on fame or power. You can decide that enough is too much and quit, as with any addiction, but there is no equivalent to physical overdose (unless we want to interpret some coronary attacks as overdosing on ambition— a by no means unreasonable argument).

In the minds of poor people—even most middle-class people—money purchases freedom. Yet real wealth addicts never avail themselves of this freedom. Perhaps this is one of the best ways to tell the addict from the nonaddict. The nonaddict coming into money uses it to expand life—to add variety, excitement, adventure, new experiences. The wealth addict, on the other hand, tends to use the money only to make more money—becoming narrower, more restricted, more single-minded.

Most wealth addicts will say they enjoy the process of amassing wealth—the satisfaction of outwitting other players at the game of sharp trading, and it's obvious that they derive *some* pleasure from it or they wouldn't do it with so much dedication, energy, and at times even enthusiasm. Yet the main pleasure in this game seems to come from the product rather than the process—from the *winning* more than the playing. Otherwise there would be far less vigilance and tension in their play.

Vigilance and joy cannot coexist. You can be elated when you win a round (although in a continuing game even elation can be a dangerous luxury), but joy is an emotion that only occurs when we let go of all watchfulness, all concern about outcomes, and simply let experience flood in and feelings flood out. Joy is incompatible with search behavior because there is nothing missing. Joy is feeling complete, full. Wealth addiction is feeling empty.

Tension, vigilance, stress, and search behavior are of course characteristic of all addictions. These are things we all share, for all of us who live short of perfect enlightenment are addicted to something—tangible or intangible, material or spiritual, concrete or symbolic. If all of us were to lose all our addictions, the advertising industry would vanish overnight and capitalism as we know it would crumble, for our society at present depends heavily upon appealing to our addictions in order to market goods. This is another way of saying that wealth addiction is of a very special order that tends to generate many others.

If you find, then, that you have difficulty relaxing, that you are restless, your eyes wander, and you have a hard time staying in the here-and-now, the chances are that you are strongly addicted to something—whatever your mind, eyes, or attention tends to shift to. If it is money, possessions, or "getting ahead," you are probably a wealth addict—especially if you find yourself accumulating possessions you don't use, getting out of touch with your body, and spending a lot of time planning and trying to control what happens to you.

In the next chapter we will take a look at those in whom these four signs of wealth addiction are writ large—some of the most severe wealth addicts in modern history. But we will make much better sense out of their behavior if we can understand what it is that ties these four signs of wealth addiction together. To do this we need to examine the role played in each of us by what I will call the Ego.

I like to look at the human organism as if it were a whole society. Writers throughout history have done it the other way around—talking of society as if it were an organism—and have often been roundly criticized for using a metaphor that left out

conflict. Today this criticism seems absurd, for it assumes that
we as individuals are without conflict. Yet we know that every
human organism is fraught with internal dissension. If it were
not, there would be no illness, no pain, no mental stress,
indecision, muscular tension, rigidities, blind spots, repression, willpower, guilt, shame, regret, New Year's resolutions,
ambition, inconsistency, and so on—most of what makes a
human being different from an animal is the result of internal
disagreements and complexities.

In spite of this, people want to think of themselves as having
some sort of individual unity. Like the American diplomats
who spoke of "American policy in Vietnam" during the 1960s
as if the populace were unanimously behind that policy, we
each like to present a united front to the world. Most of us are
aware that this unanimity rarely if ever exists within a community, or even within an individual. Yet we love to pretend that
it does. We act surprised when people are inconsistent, capri-
cious, or express some profound contradiction in their lives.
Journalists, biographers, and literary critics love to clack over
these "paradoxes of the soul" as if they occurred only in the
lives of the famous, while the rest of us went about our daily
lives with perfect internal consensus.

Why *do* we pretend to be surprised? What part of me wants
to believe that I act and speak as one undivided entity? What
part of me is analogous to the political leader who talks of
"national policy"?

In every human organism there is a special component that
concerns itself with the issue of individual survival and external threat. Biologically this special protector isn't particularly
important—from the point of view of the species, after all, the
individual organism is just an errand boy for a bit of DNA—
but obviously it can be important to the individual. I call this
protective component the "Ego," for although the word is
used by many people in many ways, this is close to what most
people seem to mean by it. Many people (especially urban
intellectuals) identify themselves so totally with this protector

that they have difficulty thinking of it as a mere part. For them it is the very core of their being. This, of course, is just what the Ego wants. For this is the part that wants to see the whole organism as in unanimous agreement. And now we see why: like the political leader, it wants to be obeyed.

The Ego is the part of us that doesn't live in the here-and-now. It's the part that stands aside and comments on what we do and feel. It lives in the past and future: critiquing what has gone before, planning and anticipating what is to come. It's the sum total of everything in us that interferes with spontaneity. It's the part of us that chatters constantly in our heads and makes meditation so difficult; that makes us pretend to ourselves and others that we are different from what we are and that we feel different from what we feel; that instructs us how not to get hurt or make fools of ourselves—how to respond "appropriately"; that gives us formulas for successful living; that pushes us to work when we feel like playing, rest when we feel like racing, expand when we feel like contracting, contract when we feel like expanding. It's a well-meaning bully—very logical and very stupid.

The human organism as a whole perceives and responds flexibly to the world on a multiplicity of levels, with great sensitivity and creativity. The Ego, on the other hand, is a simple-minded binary mechanism. All of its intricate thought processes are mere elaborations on one distinction: threat versus no-threat. Digital computers are modeled on the Ego. When people argue that a computer can't think, they're saying, in effect, "there's more to thought than the calculated fribblings of the Ego." And when computer scientists argue that some computers do in fact think they're saying, in effect, "not for *me* there isn't."

Now, to say that the Ego is simple-minded is confusing to some people. What could be more complicated than the products of conscious, logical thought? Yet such thought is ultimately accessible to us, while the human organism as a whole is largely a mystery. We can tinker with it and produce certain

effects with mediocre reliability, but most of its everyday func-
tioning—the basis of its integrity, its self-equilibrating processes, what motivates it, why it dies, why it chooses to get sick
or well at a particular time—still eludes us. The Ego can make
things *look* complex—can even make *itself* look complex, but
compared with the unconscious, or a human organism as a
whole, the Ego, or the most complicated machine ever modeled after it, is kindergarten stuff.

Yet most of us are ruled, with varying degrees of authoritarianism, by our Egos. How did this come about? How did such
a simpleton get such tight control over something so subtle
and complex as the human organism?

The answer is as old as history: in times of great danger that
simple mechanism is just what the doctor ordered. When a
rhinoceros is bearing down on us the larger questions no
longer seem important. We want simple binary answers—like
run or don't run, left or right, safe or not safe. And the Ego
is superbly gifted at processing this kind of information. In
times of stress we give the Ego dictatorial powers.

But alas, as history so often reminds us, power is heady stuff.
Which is to say it goes to the head and stays there, along with
everything else. Palaces are cozy, and when the time comes for
Cincinnatus to go back to his farm he starts to hem and haw.
He forgets to pack. He finds excuses. The state of emergency
is prolonged, and martial law becomes a way of life.

Some Egos are more despotic than others, but they all like
to restrict and control information. Every organism has an
information system that doesn't involve the Ego, but from the
Ego's point of view it is too loose, too flexible, too spontaneous, too democratic. The Ego likes to streamline and simplify
this system and redesign it on a binary basis. Only "relevant"
information gets to the palace at all—the rest is ignored. Despots hate negative feedback, because it always includes the
message that they are arrogating too much power to themselves, creating a top-heavy, overcentralized structure with an

ever-narrowing power base—a message they obviously don't want to hear. We call this shutting off of critical information "repression," whether it occurs at the political or the psychological level. Any lack of communication between our unconscious and the Ego—forgetting dreams, being out of touch with certain feelings, "motivated errors," and so on—betrays a despotic Ego.

Psychological repression, in other words, is nothing more or less than tyranny on the individual level. Kings of old were wont to kill messengers who brought bad tidings. Modern rulers are a little less crude than this, although they still manage to delude themselves quite handily. At the individual level, however, we are far more primitive in our authoritarianism. Messengers that tell us our actions are ill advised (we give these messengers names like "pain," "hurt," "suffering") are often slain on the spot, with tranquilizers, "painkillers," alcohol, barbiturates, willpower, amusements, or anything else that will allow us to go on doing what we're doing without having to learn from our mistakes.

To compensate for starving themselves of feedback, despots and despotic Egos create their own elaborate information system, with spies, informers, and so on (at the individual level these informers are represented by such things as thermometers, Rorschachs, X-rays, and other such devices, whose use is a vivid declaration of the Ego's lack of communication with the rest of the organism). But this doesn't solve the problem, since the information is always funneled through a simple binary grid that merely warns of immediate threats to the despot's power. It never tells the Ego-despot about the fundamental mistakes he's making, nor about the long-range, subtle changes that are undermining his position. The Ego's grid isn't designed to catch that information, although the body's (country's) grid may already have caught it. They say you never hear the artillery shell that hits you, and a despot always designs an information system that ignores the change that topples his regime.

Meanwhile, to maintain its position, the Ego must continue to create a sense of crisis and emergency. This is relatively easy—a state of martial law or military preparedness will usually provoke some kind of disturbance and always fosters an atmosphere of tension. The Ego adds to this atmosphere by continually pointing out and advertising dangers. This it can do with an air of sincerity since it makes no distinction between threats that endanger the whole organism and those that merely endanger the Ego. The Ego-despot argues that if he were deposed the country would be plunged into chaos, and tries to centralize control to the point where the argument becomes true. (The Shah of Iran, shortly before he fell, was said to believe that "by giving the population a deep draught of chaos it might realize that he is the only source of order in Iran.") He recognizes no such thing as the rights of citizens since he equates himself and the nation. The army is first and foremost a palace guard. There is no loyal opposition. To oppose the despot is unpatriotic. Dissent is treason. Fear of external threat and fear of internal threat become indistinguishable. This is what we call "anxiety": the Ego's fear of being deposed disguised as fear of an outside threat.

Obviously, when things reach this pass the Ego is no longer a capable leader and spokesperson for the organism, but is acting in opposition to many of the organism's best interests—becoming blind, rigid, and cruel, to the point where the organism is not only in constant stress and misery, but also in increasing danger. In other words, at some point the Ego stops being effective even in the function that originally justified its despotism. Its rigidity makes it unable to adapt to changing conditions, and its narrowness makes it unable to absorb necessary information. At this stage the Ego is a flop even in its function of protecting the organism from danger. As always happens when one person sets up to be another's protector, the protector has become the most serious threat.

This is the situation in which most of us find ourselves. At some point early in life we called in the Marines and now we can't get rid of them. Our Egos keep us in a state of fear by reminding us continually of obsolete dangers. We keep ourselves in a state of chronic mobilization because we cannot distinguish our fear of outside danger from the Ego's fear of having to give up some of its excessive control. Most human organisms seem to be deeply in need of democratization.

Rigidity is weakness, and a dictatorial Ego can be considered a weak one. The average Ego, for example—that puny Mussolini of the soul—goes all to pieces over contradictions. Everything must be either "A" or "not-A." Hence it often finds itself severely handicapped in action—since the world outside is full of contradictions. Not to mention the organism itself, which is capable of a complexity of response appropriate to its environment. So here we have a complex organism and a complex environment mediated by an imbecile. No wonder it's nervous all the time!

But Mussolini made the trains run on time, and psychologists and psychiatrists tend to look upon an Ego that gets us to the train on time as a competent one, while an Ego that consistently fails to do this is described as a "weak one." This may be a useful distinction for some purposes, but in my usage the Ego that always gets you there on time and the one that *never* gets you there on time are both the same old Mussolini. The Ego may claim that safety lies in being uptight, punctual, and consistent. It may claim that safety lies in being slovenly, disorganized, and helpless. It doesn't really matter—it's the same despot giving the orders, "protecting" you from dangers that have long since vanished, and thereby preserving its position of dominance.

I suggested that human organisms seem to be in need of

democratization. What does this mean at the individual level? The power of every ruler rests ultimately on the support—passive or active—of the people, but who are "the people" when we're talking about a single organism? Following American political parlance I use the word "Constituents" to describe everything in the human organism that is *not* the Ego: the body, impulses, desires, feelings, moods, dreams, trance, telepathy, fantasy, the "unconscious," the kind of spontaneous action involved in something like surfing or biking or free-form dancing or musical improvisation—everything that doesn't involve will or calculation.

Western peoples, who are burdened with especially dictatorial Egos, tend to look down on their Constituents and see them as somehow "lower" than their Egos—a mistake that is costing them dearly with each passing decade and may in the end be fatal to the species. Many Westerners have a hard time even imagining what a democratic personality (that is, one in which the Ego played only its proper role of Lookout or Secretary of Defense) would look like. In their minds, an Ego-less organism would simply blunder about stupidly until it died, incapable of learning or development.

Yet in the absence of acute and overwhelming danger most organisms could function quite nicely without an Ego. Nor is the Ego necessary for learning; it merely makes learning quicker and more superficial. Constituent learning is by trial and error; it is slow, sure, subtle, and deep. Things learned in this way are accepted "wholeheartedly"—that is, by the whole organism—and never forgotten. Yet at the same time they are more open to modification by experience. The Ego, on the other hand, learns by generalizing and making rules for itself. This learning is rapid because it can be quickly applied to new circumstances: having learned for some good reason to avoid one man with blue eyes, you can extend that learning to *all* men with blue eyes. (Constituent learning is not so easily extrapolated: only blue-eyed men that look, sound, and smell the same as the first would be avoided.) This advantage is also a weakness, however, since you may have nothing to fear from other men with blue eyes. Ego-learning has no fine tuning. And once a principle like this is learned it is often difficult to modify through experience (especially if the experience is avoided). An organism with a despotic Ego is like a bureaucracy (not too surprisingly, since bureaucracies are modeled after such organisms): once a rule is laid down it often develops a life of its own—sometimes a virtual immortality. Rules proliferate, conflict with each other, are often inapplicable to a given situation, are used arbitrarily, are forgotten, subverted, and so on. Obviously, each of these systems of learning has advantages and disadvantages. Constituent or trial-and-error learning is slow and clumsy but has the advantage of being closer to the firing line and hence more flexible and more finely tuned to the environment.

For a supposedly democratic people we have a touching faith in centralized, authoritarian systems. Some years ago research at M.I.T. showed that such systems work well only under simple and static conditions. When a system has to deal with complex and changing circumstances it works more efficiently if it is democratically organized. A conventional army, fighting on a conventional battlefield under traditional rules, will perform best if centralized; but a guerrilla army can survive only if it is *de*centralized. Centralized leaders have to process too much information to respond to subtle changes. Half the journalists in America, for example, seem to know when one of our pet foreign dictators is about to fall, long before the news reaches the upper echelons of the State Department or the CIA.

The stubborn myopia of political leaders is what we call "neurosis" at the individual level—the Ego's inability to discard an outmoded, irrelevant, destructive, costly, and stupid policy that once seemed like a brilliant maneuver and has become a treasured habit, a "cornerstone." When I talk of democratizing the personality (or the nation, for that matter) it isn't because democracy or decentralization is morally superior, but because it's more flexible and efficient under changing conditions.

Let's return now to the question of wealth addiction. What ties the four signs of wealth addiction together is that they are all symptoms of an overcentralized organism, a despotic Ego. They express an inability to trust Constituent learning and an exaggerated need for control on the part of the Ego.

The closing hand, for example—the fear of letting go, losing; the need to cling, ensure, stockpile—is obviously the Ego at work, guarding against an imagined future danger, unwilling to trust its Constituents to meet a future scarcity and deal with it when it arises. Such scarcities, surprises, losses, emergencies are the door to learning and growth, but the Ego is unwilling to let the Constituents grope their way through such a crisis, since its own dictatorial position would be compromised by such learning. Public ignorance is the midwife of despotism.

Confusion about goals—getting out of touch with your own wishes and needs and getting swept up in Moneythink—is also a sign of a tyrannical Ego, one that has stopped listening to its Constituents and is obsessed with its own calculations. It is the Ego's business, after all, to concern itself with *means.* It has no ends of its own save the aggrandizement of its own power position. All its goals come from its Constituents and any overemphasis on means in relation to ends is therefore a sign of the Ego's despotism and insensitivity.

Increasing possession and decreasing use are in a sense just expressions of the first two signs: the Ego tries to *ensure* against future scarcity with an intensity that blots out all incoming information about what the Constituents really *desire.* The Ego provides the means, whether the end is really sought or not, and keeps itself so busy with such providing that it never hears what the Constituents' real goals are.

Tension and search behavior are also symptoms of a despotic Ego's surplus vigilance. To understand how excessive this vigilance is in most people we need only watch the behavior of animals, who often show not the slightest sign of tension or agitation in the presence of acute danger until it is virtually upon them. I remember first being struck by this in a zoo, watching a giant tortoise doggedly pursuing some long-legged bird in an aviary. The tortoise would plod up to the bird and snap at its leg. The bird would ignore the tortoise entirely until the jaws were within a few inches of its leg; then it would step aside a foot or two. My cat, a rather timid animal, will snooze indifferently in the presence of a dog or a feared competitor unless it's within attack range. A herd of gazelles will graze peacefully in the presence of lions until the lions start to run.

All this, of course, comes from long experience and habituation to the dangers involved. *But this is precisely the experience the despotic Ego will not allow its Constituents to acquire.* Such an Ego is chronically vigilant, and the more vigilant it gets the more vigilant it *needs* to be since its Constituents are being progressively weakened. The democratic Ego of the gazelle may make a fatal miscalculation one time in ten thousand. But even then the gazelle will actually have *lived* for more hours altogether than an Ego-ridden person whose experience is totally blurred and scummed over by chronic anticipation and surplus vigilance.

Dictatorial Egos are rare among animals—usually they can be found only among domesticated beasts or laboratory specimens. We call them neurotic and view them as freaks, although such behavior is virtually universal among human beings.

Animals don't know that such a thing as security exists, and in this respect their ignorance is as useful as our knowledge, for in fact complete security is not to be found in this life. Yet many people, Ego-driven, spend their whole lives searching for it—or for some other equally elusive fantasy. In this search they may accumulate countless honors, trophies, riches, or power, yet it is never enough. An overcentralized organism doesn't know what "enough" is, since the Ego has stopped listening to its Constituents altogether and keeps slaving blindly away at what it believes to be its appointed task. Let us now look at some extreme cases of such behavior.

4

Heavy Addicts and Their Children

What will you do [said Cineas]
when you have conquered all [the world]?
Why then said the king we will return,
and enjoy ourselves at quiet in our own land.
So you may now, said the philosopher,
without this ado.

THOMAS TRAHERNE

I have chosen eight men to illustrate what it means to be a Heavy Addict. They are all Americans, and all became billionaires during the twentieth century. There are no doubt others quietly accumulating today—certainly there are many outside our borders—but I chose these eight because their billionaire status has long been accepted: John D. Rockefeller, Andrew Mellon, Henry Ford, J. Paul Getty, H. L. Hunt, Howard Hughes, John D. MacArthur, and Daniel K. Ludwig.*

From time to time I'll refer to other men and women of extreme wealth when they help to illustrate a point. These I'll

---

*There are at least two reasons for the absence of women among the Heavy Addicts. One is that this is a male-dominated society in which women are discouraged from pursuing any goal that distracts them from the traditional female role of serving the needs and interests of men. The other is that women in our society are slightly less subject to monomaniacal obsessions than men, for reasons I have discussed elsewhere (see the fourth chapter of *Earthwalk*). This is only a matter of degree, however, and in the future we can expect to see a higher percentage of women in the Addict population. Those who have appeared in the past seem to display the same characteristics as male Addicts.

call "Major Addicts" to distinguish them from the eight "Heavy Addicts," although the difference is one of degree only. The word "Addict," used alone and capitalized, will refer to Major and Heavy Addicts taken together. The cutting point for putting someone in the Major Addict class is J. P. Morgan: no one in this book will be so classified unless he or she was at least as rich, in dollar terms, as Morgan was when he died. Since people are unique, generalizations about Addicts, Heavy or Major, should be taken as statements about the majority, and obviously will not necessarily apply to every individual.

It's hard to give meaning to a figure like a billion dollars. Economists are fond of saying things like: "If you put a hundred thousand dollars under your mattress every year, it would take you ten thousand years to save a billion." They are interested in how long it would take to *get* that amount of money. I'd like to start at the other end and look at what it would take to get *rid* of it.

William Randolph Hearst, who never quite made it into the billionaires' club, but might easily have done so had he been more frugal, was an outstanding candidate for the title of world's greatest spendthrift. A rich man's son, he spent every month more money than 95 percent of the people in the world make in a lifetime.

It isn't easy to spend that much money. Yet if a billionaire, earning an average of only 6 percent on his holdings, were to spend as much as Hearst and pay the government *twice* that amount in taxes (and it's a rare Addict who pays more than 40 percent of his income), he would still be *increasing* his wealth at the rate of $15 million a year! Here is one thing we run across frequently in studying the lives of the very rich: *once you've made over a hundred million dollars it's almost impossible to get rid of it, no matter how profligate, foolish, generous, or reckless you are.* When we hear of wheeler-dealers like Bernie Cornfeld or James Ling "losing their shirts" in a bear market, we need to realize that this is only relative. At the depths of his recent poverty, for example, Cornfeld was reputed to have in the neighborhood of $50 million; Edwin Land of Polaroid lost $200 million in a few months when the market declined without even losing his place among the fifty richest people in America. (There is, in fact, a strange lexicon of poverty among the very rich: "flat broke" usually means that he or she has less than $10 million, while "penniless" or "pauper" merely means "no longer a millionaire.")

This illustration points out the absurdity of a billionaire putting any energy into making money, and the baselessness of his fear that he might ever be plunged into poverty by some loss of vigilance. The truth is quite the opposite: there is almost no way a person with such wealth can ever fight free of it. But obviously we aren't dealing with realistic goals or fears here. Addicts are massively overcentralized and quite out of touch with themselves. Their mild-mannered pronouncements on the subject—quite incongruent with the frantic compulsiveness of their behavior—make it quite clear that they have no inkling of what terror makes them spend their lives rolling up huge sums of money that they have no use for.

When we examine the lives of Heavy Addicts several common characteristics emerge, most of which have already been commented upon by other writers. We'll look first at those that seemed to play some part in the accumulation of the wealth itself, then briefly at the methods they used to enrich themselves, and finally at how they deal with *being* rich—the effect of wealth on Addicts and their children.

SOCIAL CLASS

We noted earlier that the simplest and most common way to get rich is to be born that way, and three of our Heavy Addicts (Hughes, Getty, and Mellon) were themselves the children of Addicts—choosing to multiply their wealth rather than use it. None of the Heavy Addicts was ghetto-poor. Rockefeller and Ford were both fond of exaggerating their humble origins—much to the annoyance of their respective sisters—but they always had plenty to eat and the necessities of life were never in question. Rockefeller's father even loaned him money at several crucial points in his career.

The American myth talks of going from rags to riches, but the rags usually turn out to have been a slightly shabby lower-middle-class respectability. To create an Addict certain middle-class values have to be implanted early: individualism, a work ethic, a willingness to look down on others and avoid "good fellowship," an indifference to neighborhood ties and obligations. Strong ethnic membership is a great obstacle to the development of such values—you need at least one parent who will teach you to squelch your feelings, work hard, and look after number one. It helps if that parent is, was, or has pretensions of being middle class—preferably WASP—and this has been true of virtually all the Addicts of the last century and a half.

A study by Sorokin in 1925 showed that the very rich tended to be native-born or from English-speaking countries, to have grown up in New England, to have had fathers who were either businessmen or farmers, and to have gone to college with more than five times the frequency of the general population. The last fifty years have produced a little more ethnicity among Addicts but the principle still holds: if you're born in a poor neighborhood you have to develop a ruthless detachment from the emotional bonds that keep other people rooted in it. This is why "good fellowship" is such a danger to the would-be social climber, and why men like Rockefeller and Ford continually inveighed against it. In poor neighborhoods people are often expected to help each other in times of trouble, and since the truly poor are always in trouble, only the determinedly cold-hearted manage to escape the collective morass.

Five of our Heavy Addicts came from families of modest means, but none was poor. Ford and Hunt came from farm families, while MacArthur was a preacher's son and Ludwig the son of a real estate agent. Only Rockefeller finished high school and none of the five went to college. Hunt, Ludwig, and MacArthur never went beyond the eighth grade. Yet all of these men could probably have had all the education they wanted. Dropping out had more to do with other Addict traits, which we'll now consider.

STARTING EARLY

Most of the Heavy Addicts started showing signs of being obsessed with money at a very early age. Rockefeller, for example, was saving his pennies from the time he was seven, and at the age of ten he loaned a neighboring farmer $50 at 7 percent interest. The fact that he made more money this way than he had hoeing potatoes for 100 hours impressed him, as well it might: a profound early lesson in the meaning of social class. Like most successful capitalists, he got his first stake from Mother Nature, stealing turkey chicks from a wild hen's nest until he had a flock which he raised and sold "for a good profit." From the earliest age he kept a careful ledger of all his money transactions, a trait he passed on to his son and grandsons.

Daniel Ludwig bought and repaired a sunken boat and chartered it at a large profit when he was only nine years old. H. L. Hunt was winning money gambling by the time he was a teenager. Howard Hughes fought a court battle in his teens to have himself declared competent to make adult contracts, and subsequently bought out his uncle's and grandparents' interests in the Hughes Tool Company, making him sole owner at the age of nineteen. Andrew Mellon was only nine when he realized that there was money to be made from the many farmers' wagons going by his house, and began selling hay and other produce at retail prices. He went to work in his father's bank at fifteen and was given major financial responsibilities by seventeen, the same age at which he started his own lumber business with a $40,000 loan from his father. He was described as not much interested in play.

J. Paul Getty bought his first stock at the age of eleven—100 shares of his father's oil company at $5 a share. His diary at that age shows a boy already obsessed with money and accumulation:

"Papa home—a quarter for my purse"; "Papa gave me 10 cents to go to the Post Office with a letter"; "Twenty cents for an errand"; "I now have about 275 marbles"; "Counted my stamp collection—305"; "another 55¢"; "Sold 12 copies of S.E.P."; "Papa gave me a dollar. Whee!"

What makes these entries particularly pathetic is that they are not those of a poor boy but of a rich one, and are relieved by so little else. In the eighteen months during which this diary was kept there is only one reference to a playmate, and his strongest memory of an adolescent trip to Europe was the prices.

Kenneth Lamott asserts that an early passion for money distinguished both the robber barons of the nineteenth century and the new rich of the twentieth century. Charles Thornton, for example, of Litton Industries, was buying land at an early age and "could cash a check in any store in town" by the time he was fourteen. Commodore Vanderbilt was only seventeen when he borrowed money from his mother to buy the boat with which he started his long career. Andrew Carnegie was fourteen when he invested in a firm making axles and iron bridges. In some cases it was necessity that made childhood end so early, but often it was a matter of choice. Addicts as a group are severely deficient in the ability to play, and most of them abandoned the attempt at the first available opportunity. This often makes them feel out of touch with (and contemptuous toward) those in whom playfulness is still alive—most Addicts have lived for so long under the state of emergency declared by their Ego-despots in childhood that it seems like normality to them.

THAT CHRONIC GREEDY FEELING

Several writers have commented on the fact that so many Addicts suffered some kind of psychological deprivation when they were children: loneliness, loss, lack of emotional fulfillment. Many suffered the early loss of a parent through death or separation. Henry Ford's mother died when he was thirteen. Howard Hughes's mother died when he was sixteen, his father a year later. Daniel Ludwig's parents were separated when he was fifteen, and he went to live with his father. Rockefeller's father was a flim-flam man who abandoned his family for long periods, reappearing unexpectedly and vanishing again without notice. He cheated his sons in money dealings as a matter of policy, and his failure to deliver a promised Shetland pony to the six-year-old Rockefeller was remembered with great bitterness sixty years later. H. L. Hunt started running away from home at twelve. Henry Ford left home at sixteen. Among recent Major Addicts: James Ling was orphaned at twelve; Clement Stone lost his father early in childhood; Charles Thornton's father deserted his mother when he was a child; Norton Simon's mother died when he was fourteen; and Joseph Hirshhorn's father died when he was very young (as a child, Hirshhorn was one of the few urban poor in the ranks of the Major Addicts).

Paul Getty—who grew up with both parents, was born rich, and was often called the richest man in America—once said, "I've never felt really rich—in the oil business others were all much richer than I was." John D. MacArthur, when asked why his life-style reflected so little of his huge wealth, spoke of being "on thin ice" for his first fifteen years in business: "When I began making money, I didn't want to change my life-style because I was afraid something might happen." Yet MacArthur never experienced serious poverty. A man who worked for H. L. Hunt once said, "No matter how much money he had, *Hunt was always poor in his own mind*," a statement that could be applied to most Addicts, all of whom seem to suffer from a profound sense of insecurity. It shows the futility of trying to cure an inner poverty by stuffing yourself with money.

The artist Delacroix once asked James de Rothschild, of the great banking family, to pose for a painting of a beggar, since he had "exactly the right hungry expression." Rothschild, who was a friend of the artist, agreed, and appeared the next day at the studio, suitably garbed in a disreputable costume. So convincing was the masquerade that a passerby gave him money.

A psychoanalyst hearing that H. L. Hunt always felt poor might attribute it to "oral deprivation," but since Hunt wasn't weaned from his mother's breast until he was seven years old his feeling of deprivation must have had deeper roots. Whatever the origin, Hunt was nipple-greedy his whole life long: he sucked so much oil out of Mother Earth that at the end of World War II he personally owned more oil than all of our wartime enemies combined.

The folklore of capitalism maintains that there is some kind of social value in greed of this sort: people tend to believe that if a man winds up with the lion's share of things he must be a lion. And in one sense this is true, for lions also have a tendency to take for themselves what others have earned. Apologists for the Heavy Addicts have labored mightily to find in them some special quality—leadership, good judgment, willingness to take risks, and the like—that would justify their great wealth. But while some of the Heavy Addicts are not without ability, it is almost impossible to find any distinguishing talent in the group as a whole. What distinguishes them as a group is their greed—a willingness and ability to take things from others—and it is by no means clear that this is a trait with great social benefits.

Since their apologists rely so heavily on the animal kingdom in their arguments, I will follow their lead, for I have often observed kittens and puppies nursing and been impressed with the fact that the greediest animals will continually leave their own nipple to push the runt off whatever nipple it has and take its place, even when there are more than enough nipples to go around. The sight of the runt sucking contentedly seems to excite a competitive response in the more dominant animals. They seem to want more than they can have at any given moment and would suck two nipples at a time if it were possible.

According to the apologists, these dominant animals are the "fittest." But in my experience the dominant kittens and puppies grow up to be just that, nothing more. I have known two kitten runts who barely survived the greed of their siblings and looked malnourished until they were weaned. Both grew up to be unusually gifted hunters and were intelligent in every way, particularly in contrast to their rather clumsy littermates. This is not surprising, for dominance is of very little value in hunting. Patience and alertness count for much more and these are traits the unaggressive runt has to learn in order to survive, while the dominant animal does not. The runt learns to find food—to spot an unused nipple the moment it's available and unnoticed, and seize it quickly to get as much as possible before being pushed off. The dominant animal doesn't learn this since it lives by taking what others have found. This, too, is a survival technique, but one that depends on others. Paradoxically, the dominant animal often lives in parasitic dependence on the submissive one, as the lion lives off the kill made by the lioness.

Dominance has the clearest survival value among domesticated animals, where food is not hunted or gathered but distributed by human beings. Our first knowledge of dominance among animals came from the study of chickens—hence the term "pecking order." *In a domesticated situation dominance is important because all other skills have been rendered irrelevant: if food is to be had for the taking, the greediest gets the most.*

The pop Darwinism of capitalist folklore views the various species as being in some kind of round robin tournament in which only one superior species will survive at the end. This, of course, is absurd, since predator and prey, parasite and host, grazer and grazed, are all mutually interdependent. Nothing that eats can afford to be too successful or it will outbalance its food supply and starve. *"Failure" is as essential to survival in nature as "success."* Nature is in a constantly shifting balance and too great success in any one segment means disaster. But in the case of domestic species this balance is maintained (insofar as it *is* maintained) by human beings, who normally slaughter the most "successful" animals first.

According to his biographer, Stanley Brown, H. L. Hunt not only loved winning—it was vitally important to him that others lose. Like the dominant puppies and kittens, Addicts often don't like the sight of anyone else getting something even if they themselves have enough. This trait was very marked in Howard Hughes and expressed itself in his need to possess people and places without using them. He hired a man to spend months in a motel room waiting for a call that never came. He had a barber and several doctors on standby for long periods of time, unable to practice their trade for anyone else but ignored by Hughes. He leased expensive homes he never used, hired 24-hour guards to keep people away, letting the lawns, pools, and gardens disintegrate. He kept at least five young starlets in mansions, with cars, chauffeurs, guards, and restaurant charge accounts, and although he never visited them himself, he hired private detectives to make sure no one *else* did.

Hughes usually spent his holidays alone, and liked to keep his staff on call, preventing them from seeing their families even though he rarely used them. On one Easter when he had promised an aide the day off, he made an emergency call to the aide at his home, insisting that he come immediately to Hughes's bungalow to catch a fly that had somehow penetrated Hughes's elaborate germ-free security system.

Needless to say, a man who couldn't stand to see his closest associates happy or comfortable was not likely to be responsive to any kind of demand from outsiders, and Hughes indulged in the most childish games to avoid meeting other people's legitimate requirements. If a film library made a special plea to have a particular film returned by a certain date, he would not only deliberately keep it overtime but make a special point of not watching it. He also loved to order food and then send it back, only to reorder it again and send it back. Perhaps the reason most Addicts have so little capacity for spontaneous play is that in all activities they are so completely obsessed with winning and losing.

This makes it difficult for most Addicts to work with others or share control. All the Heavy Addicts were ultimately self-employed. Those who had partners bought them out as soon as they could. All were reluctant to share responsibility and sought sole ownership of their businesses (or at the very least, an undisputable controlling interest). An Addict wants more than *access* to the nipple, he seems to want not to have to share it with anyone. He may be glad to sell the milk once he gets it, but he wants total control over the source.

This does not mean that the Heavy Addicts were in reality independent. Despite frequent oratorical statements about rugged individualism they were all deeply dependent on loyal and often brilliant managers. Daniel Ludwig never really got off the ground before he hired William Wagner, and Howard Hughes would probably have lost what he started with without Noah Dietrich and Robert Maheu. Henry Ford's success was due to a whole series of able associates who compensated for his own excesses and rigidities, but "like so many individualists he would not stand for individualism in others." Anyone in the Ford Company who got any publicity or recognition was promptly purged, and one by one his most capable colleagues fell away, leaving him alone with the infamous and relatively useless Harry Bennett. A despotic Ego is terrified of human interdependence, and rarely are even the most faithful and able of an Addict's lieutenants and allies rewarded appropriately for their services—often not at all.

SINGLE-MINDEDNESS

Perhaps the most common characteristic of the Heavy Addicts is their narrowness, their single-minded obsession with the goal of making money. Most people who dream of getting rich imagine all the things they could do with the money, and that very imaginativeness prevents them from making those dreams come true. Their minds are too rich to make their pockets rich. Heavy Addicts rarely seem to bother to think of what they can *do* with the money—that's just a distraction from the goal of *making* it. This is also why most Addicts have little scandal in their personal lives and tend to be "settled family men." As Kenneth Lamott observes, their "strongest lust" is the "pecuniary appetite." Goronwy Rees, in his study of European multimillionaires, emphasizes the importance of this ability to concentrate energy on a single goal, combined with complete ruthlessness and an almost total disinterest in everything except making money. After all, the kind of persistence that enabled Getty to spend twenty years acquiring control over Tidewater Oil doesn't come to people with a diversity of interests and talents.

John D. Rockefeller was perhaps the perfect example of a man with only one interest in life: "His very narrowness was an invaluable asset in driving the hardest bargain possible: he had made himself into a perfect instrument for the conduct of business, and the only pleasure he allowed himself came from success in his transactions." An acquaintance reported that the only time he had ever seen Rockefeller show any enthusiasm was when he heard a report that he had acquired some oil below the market price. He had no real friends and, in fact, taught his Sunday School class that they mustn't let "good fellowship get the least hold" on them. He had no interest in books or ideas—even the greatest works of art he saw in purely monetary terms. When he bought a pretty summer house he tried to have it double as a hotel, charging his bewildered guests for the privilege of his company. (Paul Getty tried the same thing at his Sutton Place mansion, for tax purposes.) This "amazing single-mindedness" naturally made Rockefeller a "dull and predictable" person.

Henry Ford mechanized himself in much the same way. During his early years he worked fifteen hours a day, and one of his biographers called him "a sort of human dynamo, made to run purposefully along a single track." He was obsessed with finding ways to save labor—not so people could enjoy themselves more, but so more energy would be freed to "do the job." He introduced the assembly line because it seemed wasteful to him to see men wandering around a machine shop getting tools and materials and stopping on the way to chat with one another. This "waste-motion," of course, was the only thing that made the job tolerable, but Ford, who was farseeing and socially concerned in many ways, could not understand this. Having made himself into a machine, he saw nothing wrong in doing it to millions of workers. "His mind was astonishingly simple. He could concentrate on a single idea almost as perfectly as the inmate of a State Asylum." He thought people should be as much like machines as possible and once suggested that we should be able to repair a human body just like we do a defective boiler. Like Rockefeller, he took a dim view of friendship and was opposed to the idea that people needed to have good personal relationships on the job—even that departments needed to have civil or cooperative relations: "Too much good fellowship may indeed be a very bad thing."

For Ford everything was a means. He couldn't see "any use" in dancing, for example, and called it a "waste of effort" and "aimless, just moving around to music." Only when he realized that it would be useful in courting his future wife did he show interest. He once claimed that "the unhappiest man on earth is the one who has nothing to do"—a statement which holds for Addicts, if for no one else.

Perhaps the most extreme case of a single-track mind was Howard Hughes, who instructed his staff that they could only discuss subjects that he himself had introduced—a good example of how a despotic Ego resists negative feedback. His reason was revealing, for to an extent it characterizes all the Heavy Addicts: "I just can't concentrate on more than one subject at a time."

Often this single-mindedness expresses itself in what Goronwy Rees calls an "extraordinary capacity for hard, concentrated, and continuous work," with little taste for pleasure or recreation. The Addict's indulgence in what most people imagine to be the diversions of the rich tends to be a concession to what the world expects of him, and if he really lets himself become engaged in them they quickly become transformed into profit-making enterprises: "His pleasures are simply the continuation of business by other means."

Max Gunther also speaks of "worship" of work by Addicts, although many "admit quite frankly that their compulsion to work has destroyed their marriages and hurt their relationships with their children and perhaps damaged other components of their personal lives." Yet they show no inclination to mend their ways. Daniel Ludwig claims to have no interest in anything but business, and having "few friends and no hobbies, he seems to concentrate more and more on work as he gets older"—"if he admires the view it's with the eye of a developer." Paul Getty regularly worked until three or four in the morning, often going for eight hours without eating or resting, and forcing his managers to do the same. Philip Armour, the meat-packing millionaire, used to arrive at his plant as early as 4:00 A.M. William Lear, manufacturer of the Lear jet, worked every day of the year. James Ling, who put together the LTV conglomerate, works a 90-hour week. Charles Thornton of Litton Industries is quoted as saying "I can't stand useless leisure." H. L. Hunt, who regularly worked six days a week, described as his "most memorable" Christmas one on which he spent the entire day working. Ray Kroc of hamburger fame "seems to enjoy working for its own sake." But in fact all this work is directed toward a goal, however symbolic, ethereal, and unrewarding that goal may be. H. L. Hunt summarized his life accurately when he said, "Everything I do I do for a profit."

Alfred Krupp, of the German munitions empire, was so obsessed with work that he built his home in the middle of his steel works—the better to keep an eye on the factory at all times. He refused to go to concerts or other entertainments on the grounds that no music could be as sweet to his ears as the sounds of steel being produced. His wife was a virtual prisoner in this nightmarish environment, and one wonders what she thought of the joys of great wealth as she saw her fine linens destroyed by grit and her delicate glasses shattered by the constant shocks of the steamhammers.

Judge Thomas Mellon, after the perfunctory and completely loveless courtship of his future wife had proved successful, commented that had he been refused, his only regret would have been the loss of time involved. Like Ford and Rockefeller, he advised his sons against having friendships with either sex, and in the case of Andrew, at least, the lesson was well learned, for Mellon "loved the manipulation of millions with an intensity that no woman could inspire." This was depressing to his wife Nora, a healthy, life-loving woman who sat night after night alone or with her children while Andrew, "locked in his study, nursed his dollars, millions of dollars, maddening dollars, nursed larger and bigger at the cost of priceless sleep, irretrievable health, and happiness—dollars that robbed him and his family of the time he could have devoted far more profitably to a mere 'Thank God, we are living.' " More spirited than Frau Krupp, she finally divorced him.

A reporter for the Chicago *Tribune* once set out to interview a number of very rich men for their advice to the ambitious and was amazed to find that they were all in their offices when he called, hard at work. He concluded that the real secret of getting rich, though none of the men had mentioned it, was "be compulsive."

DETAILS, DETAILS

Being compulsive means many things, of course, and one of them is a preoccupation with detail. Rees expresses amazement that the Addict seems to violate every principle of good management—that instead of confining himself to larger matters of corporate strategy in his far-flung enterprises, he tends to get "absorbed in the often trivial, often dreary, but to him inexhaustibly fascinating details." Perhaps, as Rees suggests, it's having their own money at stake that keeps them from displaying the sweeping detachment of the corporate manager, but whatever the reason, the Addict is "not much interested in broad principles and policies; it is the microscopic meticulousness of his field of vision that surprises." He has the "miser's capacity for counting the smallest coin."

Rockefeller was one of the most notorious of these penny-pinchers. After he had put together the Standard Oil Trust he still spent much time prowling around the corners of his empire, looking over ledgers and making suggestions to foremen. One of these was that 39 drops of solder, instead of 40, should be used in the construction of kerosene cans. Then, of course, there was the famous memo to a foreman about 750 missing bungs, which Rockefeller had discovered in going through inventory reports. Since the missing bungs were worth less than a dollar altogether, it's clear that Rockefeller placed a very low value on his own time and labor. "He was obsessed with minutiae . . . even more than by the great matters of the Standard."

Daniel Ludwig once personally checked every sounding on a navigation chart of Las Minas Bay, Panama, using a rented motorboat, a 20-cent roll of string, and a 5-cent bolt. Ludwig is extremely reluctant to delegate authority and tends to get involved in decisions at all levels of his huge and complex empire. A "frugal man who will risk millions while pinching pennies," he once went so far as to try to find ways of storing oil in the hollow masts of his ships. Paul Getty was also described as a man "obsessed with detail," who felt obliged to make a "microscopic examination" of the costs of his Sutton Place residence. G. F. Swift, the multimillionaire meat-packing king, used to prowl around his plant looking in the sinks for signs of grease. Gulbenkian, the oil tycoon, got into a $10 million lawsuit with his son—a suit for which the legal fees alone cost $80,000—because the latter charged a $4.50 lunch to the company. Ray Kroc checks individual McDonald's parking lots for litter. Henry Ford intruded himself personally into the most trivial plant economies.

Howard Hughes once scolded a propman for buying a whole chicken for a film scene in which an actress had to chew on a drumstick. He would spend hours stacking and restacking piles of papers so that their edges didn't stick out. He spent $30,000 a year keeping a guard on a dilapidated, unflyable plane because it contained a sport jacket with $17,000 in the pocket. He gave elaborate instructions on how to sweep broken glass off stairs, what kind of brassiere an actress should wear (this necessitated a long rambling memo about the positioning of her nipples), and how fast drivers should go over bumps when chauffeuring starlets around (he was concerned that too much bouncing would cause sagging breasts). A typist once typed the same letter for him two hundred times, working with him from midnight to 7:00 A.M.

Naturally, all this took his energies away from major policy questions. During the 1950s, when all the airlines were converting to jets, TWA almost collapsed because Hughes took so long looking over design details of various planes. Whenever indecision began to overwhelm him he would spend days stacking and restacking boxes of Kleenex. During a crisis in

Hughes Aircraft, when his managers were tearing their hair and begging him for a major decision, he asked them to look into proceeds from the plant's vending machines.

It may seem strange that these heavily overcentralized personalities—Ego-driven, single-minded, and so on—should be so concerned with trivia. Since they are so focused, so concentrated, shouldn't they be attuned to the larger trends, the broad sweep of events? Unfortunately, despotism exists not to make an organism or society more efficient, but to give the despot a greater feeling of control. An Addict pores over details because it creates an illusion of control over events. The details are so small they make the Ego feel big: divide and conquer. Nothing of any value is accomplished through all this work. It's merely a tranquilizer, reassuring the Ego that it really *is* in control so that it can calm down enough to deal with at least some portion of life's real complexity. We have to remember that Addict Egos are too simple to deal with all the fluid complexity of either the real world or their own bodies. In constant terror they can only reassure themselves by ignoring most of that complexity, concentrating on one fairly simple fragment—money—and putting all their energy into gaining power over that fragment. Details—especially simple, mechanical, quantifiable, man-made ones—are very comforting because they *can* be controlled. Anyone, after all, can stack Kleenex boxes or add figures. Coping with anything as complex as living beings is quite another matter. Hewins's remark about Paul Getty could probably be applied to any Addict: "Where he seems to fail is over the mysteries, the intangibles and imponderables."

CAUTIOUS GAMBLERS

The Heavy Addicts are extremely cautious people. They look ahead, hoard their money, and hedge their bets. They like to have control over everything that affects their operation—to buy out not only their partners but also their suppliers and distributors, so that nothing is left to chance or the whims of other people. Judge Mellon advised that "a man ought never to risk much."

Yet most of the Heavy Addicts, somewhere along the line, took a risk. John D. Rockefeller withdrew with a shudder from the chaotic and chancy oil-producing business, yet in the early days of the creation of Standard Oil (since he always started with his most powerful competitors and worked down) he would have been destroyed had he run up against one honest man. Once he controlled 95 percent of the refining industry he never needed to take another chance, and he never really did.

Some such moment can be found in the life of every Addict. Goronwy Rees is quite correct in saying that the Addict combines a miser's caution with a gambler's recklessness. Heavy Addicts don't really like to gamble when there's too much at stake but at some point in their lives they take a gamble, ride it, and get off as soon as they can buy the game and run it by their own fail-safe rules. Rarely do we find an Addict taking such a chance a second time. Rarely does he need to, for once you're rich, gambling is much less risky.

John D. MacArthur's early career, for example, was pretty much a failure. During the Depression he bought into an insurance firm which did so badly that MacArthur ended up sole owner because no one else wanted the stock (Ford and Ludwig had similar good-bad luck). As business improved during the postwar boom he acquired some land bargains. During the 1950s, for example, a mortgage failure dropped 6,000 acres of Palm Beach real estate in his lap, which led ultimately to his becoming Florida's largest landowner. After he became a billionaire MacArthur once lost $30 million in a bank failure, but he shrugged it off, saying "I make more than that in a year." Overall, MacArthur probably had more failures than successes, but the successes happened to be such big ones that subsequent failures could be ignored.

Daniel Ludwig's early career was also littered with failures.

For almost two decades he was just one jump in front of his creditors; his business was so insubstantial he had to use his windowsill for a desk. His subsequent success had much to do with the business upturn surrounding World War II. Now that Ludwig is rich, however, every move he makes is considered shrewd, even though he can well afford to gamble—if he makes a dozen serious blunders a year he can shrug them off like MacArthur. Two business journal articles in the 1970s described speculative enterprises of Ludwig's that seemed, on the face of it, stupid, but the authors both concluded that they must be smart or Ludwig wouldn't have made them. It may be some years before we know whether or not Ludwig was right. The point is that a rich man can afford to play such long shots.

Another advantage to being rich is that your predictions become self-fulfilling prophecies. When a billionaire invests, others take note and begin to invest, too; ambitious people are attracted to the enterprise and want to work for it. Conversely, when an Addict withdraws money from an enterprise, others follow suit, and it may well collapse. At that point the Addict will be said to have a shrewd knowledge of business trends. Hetty Green, for example, decided in 1907 that the men in a certain bank were "too good-looking." She withdrew her money and advised her friends to do likewise. The next day there was a run on the bank and it failed, adding to Green's already enormous reputation as a canny Wall Street prophet. If Ludwig proves to be right, it may have more to do with his reputation than with his judgment.

People like to have heroes, but if any of the Addicts had been right more than half the time there would have been a lot fewer of them, for most of them made their fortunes by grabbing opportunities other Addicts had scorned. Rockefeller thought oil production—the industry that made Hunt and Getty rich— was made for fools and losers. J. P. Morgan thought General Motors was a poor investment. And virtually every Addict in the country thought Henry Ford was crazy when he announced that he was going to share some of his profits with his workers in 1914. The success of this move in creating a mass market for his cars made him a new business oracle, yet his own blindness to the public demand for variety in car models later cost him the leadership of the automobile industry.

H. L. Hunt's early efforts at land and cotton speculation were disastrous, and even in the oil business he did poorly for a long time. He lost money in his Florida land speculations and was deeply in debt during most of his early life. On more than one occasion he was saved from bankruptcy by a poker game.

Howard Hughes sold the Hughes Tool Company for $300 million less than it was worth. In the early 1950s Hughes Aircraft was such a shambles as a result of his "notorious indecision" that the Secretary of the Air Force attacked him for jeopardizing American defenses. In 1961 he lost control of TWA and was sued for mismanagement. TWA's stock was then $13 a share, but by the time he was actually ordered by the court to sell, the company had had a new management for five years and the stock was close to an all-time high of $86 a share. As a result of losing a protracted lawsuit Hughes was half a billion dollars richer—surely the most money ever made at one time through failure. This was a man popularly considered to be a "financial wizard." Yet he fought bitterly against losing TWA, spending millions to avoid what turned out to be the source of almost half his fortune.

Indeed, the only things Hughes owned that did well were the ones he never touched. He lost $20 million for RKO and was sued by the other stockholders, but by the time he decided to cut his losses and sell out, the TV networks started buying old movies and he made a big profit from the rising stock. He got $60 million in war contracts without ever delivering a single plane.

Kenneth Lamott, puzzling over the problem of how Hughes managed to get so rich, concludes that, under certain circumstances, "money will tend to multiply itself without rational

control and even in spite of gross errors and eccentricities that
outrage not only every accepted principle of good business
management but also the advice of common sense."

People are reluctant to allow for luck in matters of this kind.
A trapper, asked what was going on at an oil drilling site,
responded, "Some silly son of a bitch is looking for oil on the
north flank." When activity at the site increased, the same
question elicited a slightly modified reply: "Some smart son of
a bitch found oil on the north flank." People love to feel that
human beings are in control of the environment, even if it
means attributing clairvoyance to every gambler who wins.

Economic forces are creating large fortunes all the time—
every time there's a bull market a new crop of multimillionaires is created—usually from among those who have a
good deal to start with. Someone, for example, has to own the
land on which a new city is built or in which oil, gold, silver,
diamonds, or uranium is found, and the possession of this land
need not entail any special vision. When a boom hits, it increases the value of what people are holding, and those who
hold the most reap the most benefit. Those who are poorest
and own nothing reap nothing. The wealthy have the capital
to exploit opportunities while the poor do not. Many a poor
man or woman has had a million-dollar idea, or the wit to buy
into something when it was cheap, but hasn't had the wherewithal to do it.

When the downturn occurs, furthermore, and prices fall,
the poor have to sell at a loss, but the rich do not. Their
wealth on paper may decrease markedly but they can ride
out the storm until prices go up again. If making money is
buying cheap and selling dear, then the rich obviously have
a great advantage: when it's time to sell dear, they have
something to sell—the poor do not; and when it's time to
buy cheap, they have the money to buy with—the poor do
not. "Them as has, gits" is not just a bitter saying—it's an
economic law.

A final word: we may admire Heavy Addicts because they

took a risk, but it's easy to forget, in a society like ours, that of all the risks you can take, money is one of the least important. When you lose it, after all, you lose nothing real, and at some level people know this ("it's only money"). There are many risks in life, many ways of living successfully. To admire or emulate the Heavy Addict is to put yourself down—to ignore the far more significant risks you may have taken in your own life.

TECHNIQUES OF SELF-ENRICHMENT

In wealth no limit is set up within man's view;
those of us who now have the largest fortune
are doubling our efforts.
SOLON

Since all money at any given time is in someone's possession, to get rich the Heavy Addict must take the money from someone else. There are several ways of doing this: you can take the money from the poor, you can take it from the rich, or you can take it from the government—that is to say, from everyone.

Taking it from the poor is difficult in one way since they have so little. You have to take a little bit from a great many. Taking it from the rich is easier in one way since you don't have to deal with so many people, but since the rich are more attached to money it's harder to get it away from them. The poor are powerless and money can be extracted from them by compulsion in one form or another: underpaying them for their labor, using their land or resources without compensation, selling them overpriced goods or services under monopolistic conditions, saving money at their expense by cutting corners on safety, pollution, and so on.

The rich, on the other hand, are both powerful and vigilant. The best way to get money out of them is to exploit their addiction—to cheat them by playing on their greed. Therefore it requires more intelligence to get rich at the expense of the rich than to get rich at the expense of the poor.

The easiest way of all to get rich—and hence the one most favored among Addicts—is to take it from the government. Governments deal in huge sums of money, controlled by men who are paid rather poorly in relation to their responsibility. The complexity of bureaucracies and the necessity of their spending budgeted money or carrying out hastily conceived programs by a certain time make them ripe plums for alert pickers. A well-placed bribe can purchase small adjustments in regulations that will funnel millions into waiting hands.

Taking It from Governments

One of the most popular techniques for getting money from the government is to procure military contracts. As Lamott points out, governments never look too hard at defense industry profits during wars, when lots of money gets thrown around with maximum haste and minimum accounting. World War II contracts were virtually unaudited, while the Vietnam War, with even less fiscal supervision, saw annual defense industry profits of $4.5 billion. Although the most cursory inspections turned up scandalous practices, the public remained indifferent. Military spending always tends to benefit the rich since the proportion of the money that goes to labor is relatively small. And such spending offers unique opportunities for the Addict: first, secrecy in the name of national security may hide the most extensive corruption from public scrutiny; second, the sums of money involved are so large that huge amounts of padding can easily be tucked away in them; third, the size, scope, and, in wartime, confusion inherent in the industry make it very easy for enormous quantities of goods and money to get lost; and fourth, military products are not sold to the public or used in any productive way, but are either destroyed or declared obsolete, which makes them ideally suited to "siphoning off" of various kinds.

But the best way to extract money from the government is to avoid *giving* money to it, and most Addicts, past and present, have been successful in avoiding all but a fraction of the taxes that would ordinarily be expected from them. In a *Fortune* article Lewis Beman states flatly that "one explanation for their billionaire status is that they have been able to shelter their fortunes from the tax collector." Income tax forms are complex today because a series of loopholes have been written in, all serving in one way or another as subsidies for Addicts. The biggest change was the tax cut in 1962, described by Collier and Horowitz as a "massive redistribution of income from the poor to the wealthy." Almost half of the cut—engineered in part by David Rockefeller—went to the wealthiest 20 percent of the population.

John D. Rockefeller, Sr., called the U.S. State Department "one of our greatest helpers," enabling Standard Oil to "push our way into new markets to the utmost corners of the world." Rockefeller's executives bribed senators and other government officials with an openness not possible today, even committing the transactions to paper. They assumed that government existed to put money in their pockets and became indignant when anyone suggested that this was inappropriate. The late Howard Hughes, who made a great show of being a rugged individualist, made a sizable portion of his fortune by siphoning it from public treasuries—to the tune of over $1.5 million a *day* during his last decade—and expected government leaders to carry out his personal whims. When President Johnson asked Hughes for $25,000 for the LBJ library, Hughes refused, saying "Hell, I couldn't control the son of a bitch with $25,000." He viewed the governor and legislature of Nevada as personal servants and was so annoyed when Nevada voters neglected to elect his chosen candidate that he moved to Nassau, asking his aide Robert Maheu to "wrap that government up down there" so that it would be "a captive entity in every way."

H. L. Hunt claimed to be a father of the Connally "hot oil"

act, which limited oil production to keep prices up—one of many ways in which the federal government "smoothed Hunt's path to great wealth." The fact that so many Addicts are in the oil industry is due in considerable part to the greatest government handout of all, the oil depletion allowance.

Taking It from the Poor

No great fortune was ever made without robbing the poor in some way. The secret of getting rich is cutting corners, and some of those corners involve the flesh and spirit of disadvantaged human beings. Rockefeller money in recent years, for example, has been invested in the Consolidation Coal Company, notorious for lax safety regulations in its mines and the prevalence of black lung disease among its miners, and New England Nuclear, which was repeatedly reprimanded by the Atomic Energy Commission "for discharging potentially disastrous levels of radioactivity into the air and sewers of Boston," and caused the rapid death of an employee through exposure to plutonium. Conditions on Daniel Ludwig's tankers (which sail under Liberian and Panamanian flags) have been described (somewhat emotionally) as "hardly more humane than the ships of the African slave trade."

Miners at the Colorado Fuel and Iron Company's Ludlow mine (John D. Rockefeller, Jr.'s first solo enterprise) in 1913 were paid less than 17¢ an hour, in scrip that could be used only in company stores charging extortionate prices. They lived in two-room company shacks for which they paid exorbitant rents and from which they could be evicted on three days' notice. The churches and schools were company controlled and censored, and government and law enforcement officials were virtual employees of the company. Minimal safety regulations were not enforced and accidental deaths and injuries were common.

Today, conditions of this kind are rare in domestic American operations, although not uncommon in the Third World.

But workers are still killed and injured even in unionized plants by exposure to lethal chemicals and radioactivity, and poor people living near industrial areas still have their air and water polluted so that corporations can save money. One of the great secrets of getting rich has always been to get something for nothing—air, water, land, resources, waste disposal— and the poor are the best source for such bargains.

When John Jacob Astor died the *New York Herald* suggested that he should have left half his fortune to the people of New York, whose intelligence and enterprise had swelled the value of his property. But this interdependence is exactly what the despotic Ego is afraid to recognize. Addicts are "rugged individualists"—if you give them something they will persuade themselves that they cleverly cheated you out of it. The very term "self-made" captures the Ego's need to deny its dependence on a physical body.

Taking It from the Rich

One of the best ways of making quick money is fleecing other addicts. Rockefeller himself owed a part of his fortune to this technique: offering larceny to others but taking the biggest portion himself. He used their greed to make them subservient to his greater greed.

In the past thirty or forty years, stock market manipulators and conglomerate builders have relied heavily on this technique in building their new financial empires. This has been made possible because of the enormous propaganda machine that we voluntarily maintain as a nation, a machine that focuses all our yearnings on the accumulation of wealth and property. This tends to make marks of all of us—ready and waiting for someone to come along with a fast-money scheme. And since nature abhors a vacuum, someone always does.

People make money when other people believe money can be made. This is the Pyramid Club or Chain Letter principle: I take your money in return for showing you how to take other people's. I get rich, you *may* get rich, those you persuade will probably lose their shirts as the belief system reaches its perimeter. This was Bernie Cornfeld's method, which involved selling stock, or more precisely, selling a dream of wealth. The important thing with wealth addiction is that you can't go halfway: those who are half-hearted or trusting in their addiction are always bilked by Heavy Addicts, who think of nothing else.

An Ill Wind

Paul Getty's comment on the Great Depression expresses, as nothing else can, the difference between the way rich people and poor people experience an economic disaster: "The bargain days of 1932 and 1933 were not exploited to the full."

Kenneth Lamott advances what he calls a "Catastrophe Theory of Wealth"—that wealth addicts have become rich whenever a "natural or man-made catastrophe has upset the established order." He points out that during the desperate years from 1930 to 1933, when the number of taxpayers with incomes over $5,000 a year fell from 810,000 to only 330,000, the number of people with incomes of over $1 million increased—in one year more than doubling. Many of the Heavy Addicts simply bought freely during the "bargain days" and coasted to the top as the World War II boom inflated the value of their holdings. As Lamott observes, catastrophes have been "the midwives to our greatest fortunes," and these fortunes are usually made by people who "bet on the side of the disaster," against their fellow citizens.

To do this requires a certain cold-bloodedness. When a flood threatens, most people will be out on the levee piling up sandbags. The Addict will be buying up boats—"betting on the disaster." A millionaire developer during the London Blitz was heard to say, "Did you hear the bombs last night? There must be some bargains around this morning!" Arndt Krupp, founder of the munitions dynasty, bought up land in Essen at bargain prices from citizens fleeing the plague—the Krupp family still owns it after four hundred years.

If this seems a bit callous we must remember that Addicts as a group tend to be cut off from other people at a feeling level. Since their Egos always operate "on emergency," a community calamity has very little emotional impact. They react in a cold, single-minded, businesslike way because their whole existence is treated by their Egos as a dangerous calamity to be cured through wealth.

The most fruitful catastrophes have always been war and depression. John Jacob Astor became a millionaire by buying up Manhattan mortgages during the Panic of 1837. The Rothschilds got their start during the Napoleonic Wars. Commodore Vanderbilt got rich chartering near-defunct ships to the government during the Civil War. And during World War I, DuPont annual profits were 26 times what they had made in the best of their preceding years. Nor was this unique to munitions-makers. The number of millionaires quadrupled during World War I, while the number of multimillionaires multiplied more than six times. Paul Getty was well aware of his debt to both World Wars and the Depression in accumulating his riches. Hughes, Hunt, and Ludwig all owed much of their wealth to World War II.

Most of the great American fortunes of the last century were made by selling defective goods to the Union armies: disintegrating clothes and blankets, boots made of paper, meat from diseased cattle and hogs, guns that wouldn't shoot or blew up in the soldiers' hands. Vanderbilt, J. P. Morgan's father, Fisk, Armour, the DuPonts, Rockefeller, Judge Thomas Mellon, and many others got rich from the Civil War. Not all of these fortunes were based on shoddy goods, but all were based on a sharp division of labor between soldiers and moneymakers, for most Addicts have successfully avoided military service. Daniel Drew served briefly in the War of 1812, which makes

him "unique [among] all the early great American capitalists. . . ." and, according to Kenneth Lamott, the same division
of labor exists today. During the Civil War some of Judge
Mellon's sons showed an interest in joining up but he told
them only "greenhorns" enlist, adding that "there are plenty
of other lives less valuable." They listened, and the whole
family made handsome profits out of it. Rockefeller also felt
that his business could not suffer his absence. Lamott concludes that "the great American fortunes were founded in
times of danger and confusion and nourished by the blood of
young men." We might say of all Addicts what Rockefeller's
sister Lucy said of him: "When it's raining porridge you'll
always find John's bowl right side up."

Things are pretty much the same today. In 1978—a year
in which inflation and unemployment pushed millions of
Americans into abject poverty and made middle-income
people feel the pinch so badly that they mounted a tax revolt—the profits of many major corporations soared to re-
cord heights. And between 1970 and 1975—a period that
most Americans experienced as hard times economically—
the number of people with annual incomes of a million dollars or more doubled.

LIVING IN EL DORADO

Wealth is the diploma of slavery.
SENECA

People dream of "making it." But what do they do when
they "arrive"? Most Addicts act as if they hadn't noticed: "It
seems almost an axiom that [though] the rapidly rich . . . often
complain about their limited playtime, almost all the *nouveaux*
share a drive to accumulate assets beyond any expectation of
liquidating the lucre." One recent millionaire suggested that
"somebody ought to give a correspondence course on what to
do with sudden wealth." Another complained that "one really

needs two lives. One to get to the top. The other to enjoy it all."

This doesn't mean Addicts are unaware of the fact that they have enough money to meet all their needs: they know *when* to stop, they just don't know *how*. Cyrus Eaton, for example, remarks that there are "fairly circumscribed limits to the purely personal gratifications great wealth can procure." Millionaire William Riley: "After a certain point increased earnings will not raise your standard of living." Henry Ford: "I shall never use what I have. . . . Money doesn't do me any good. I can't spend it on myself." John W. MacKay and H. L. Hunt both said that someone with $200,000 was as well off personally as they were with their many millions. Most others have picked a million dollars as a good round figure. As Joseph Hirshhorn observes: "The money doesn't matter—not after the first million. How could it? You can't wear more than two shirts a day, or eat more than three meals."

Yet they keep on making more, and rationalize it in various ways. Hirshhorn, for example, says he does it "just to test my judgment," and for James Ling it's "only the way you keep score." But these are half-truths. You can test your judgment playing backgammon or mountain climbing or driving a car in the city. These men understand quite clearly that money is purely symbolic, but they slide over the fact that they are fiercely addicted to that symbol. It is true that they often have little interest in what the money can buy—they're interested in demonstrating their ability to *make* it—a kind of financial potency. Henry Ford is often held up as a billionaire who cared nothing for money, yet when he was running his farm he "never failed to sell an animal for more than he had paid for it," and his original humanitarian interest in developing a tractor was quickly put aside when he found that there was a better market for a horseless carriage. People mistake indifference to the *use* of money for indifference to money itself.

There are a few Addicts who have tried to stop. Andrew Carnegie, for example, promised himself in writing at the age of thirty-three never to make more than $50,000 a year, an income he had just achieved. He swore he would retire at thirty-five and use his surplus wealth to help the poor, but it was thirty years before Carnegie sold out for half a billion dollars and started giving his money away, commenting that "the man who dies rich dies disgraced." Paul Getty thought in his twenties that a million dollars was all the money he needed and tried for a year to stop accumulating. But the need was too strong and he died with more than a thousand times that amount. One of the few known Addicts to kick the habit was Gerard Lambert, the man who, a half-century ago, invented bad breath and got rich by making millions of people neurotic about their body odors. While still a comparatively young man he became bored with making money and retired to seek more amusing pastimes, leaving a whole nation with a bad taste in its mouth.

Some Addicts have learned to scale down their addiction because of ill health or hard economic conditions. When *The Wall Street Journal* did an 18-year follow-up on a group of new entrepreneurs they had studied in 1960 they discovered that several had gone bankrupt in the late 1960s recession and at least one seemed to have profited by it: "When I was worth $50 million, I wanted $100 million. When I was down to a few million, I discovered it was only paper and no big deal. . . . I got rid of my big yacht and my million-dollar house. Now I got a couple of sailboats and a $250,000 house, and I like 'em just as well."

But most Addicts not only keep on making money—they also keep on saving it. When we consider that the gifts of some of the most famous American philanthropists scarcely made a dent in their great fortunes it seems surprising that the Heavy Addicts would hesitate to buy goodwill at such a bargain. Yet, although there are well-known philanthropists among the Major Addicts, only two of our eight billionaires were involved in philanthropy to any extent. H. L. Hunt was blackballed at the Dallas Country Club because of his curt refusals to give to any charities, and lost the political influence he sought because his contributions were so nominal. Asked to contribute to the restoration of a church at his birthplace, Hunt sent five dollars. His son, Bunker—also a billionaire—has also been criticized for his lack of interest in charity. Getty and Hughes were notorious nongivers, and Ludwig and MacArthur are certainly not known for their philanthropies. Henry Ford did less with his wealth than his partner Couzens, who had less than a tenth as much to do it with. Nor is this a peculiarity of American Addicts. Rees observes that "surprisingly" few European men of extreme wealth are involved in philanthropy, and that the amount that "even the greatest philanthropists have given away out of their tax-free income [probably] would not amount to a fraction of the tithe the Church once expected of every Christian, however poor." Even the Rockefeller gifts— though large in an absolute sense—made no appreciable impact on the family fortune, and involved no personal sacrifice. Nelson Rockefeller's Albany Mall, built with public money as a monument to himself, cost the taxpayers almost as much as the *combined* philanthropies of John D. Rockefeller, Sr., and John D. Rockefeller, Jr.

But we must not assume that Heavy Addicts, so ungenerous with the public, are any more generous with themselves. Brown says of H. L. Hunt that "he enjoyed neither spending it nor giving it away": If his guests got drugstore sandwiches for lunch, with typewriter paper for a napkin he was just as frugal with himself—wearing worn clothes, cracked shoes, and a clip-on tie, trimming his own hair and eating brown-bag lunches. And if Getty had a pay phone in his home and had to be "badgered" to send his eldest son a wedding present, he was also willing to wait an hour for a ride in someone else's car rather than spend a few shillings on a taxi.

John MacArthur, with his "baggy wash-and-wear slacks," looked "less like a billionaire than like a retired postal clerk whose social security check is being stretched too thin. . . . Some people would be surprised if MacArthur spent even as much as $172 a month on himself." He saved cigarette butts and once called an executive meeting so he could serve up some leftover baked beans that had been burned at an employee picnic the day before, disguised with a "special syrup." Howard Hughes owned no clothes at all during his last decade, except pajamas, undershorts, a robe and slippers, and ate Campbell's soup while his aides banqueted. Collis Huntington, the railroad king who left $75 million, spent less than $200 a year on himself until he married.

Every waiter knows that wealthy customers are the worst tippers, and Edmund Bergler points out that even those who spend freely in public are often "merciless misers" at home. John Jacob Astor, when he was "too old to walk and had to be tossed in a blanket to get his circulation going," hounded his rental agent to pursue a penniless woman for her rent until the agent in desperation got the money from Astor's son. Cornelius Vanderbilt lived in a small, shabby house with his wife and twelve children, and "watched the domestic food budget as if he were the overseer of an orphanage." He was still pinching pennies on his deathbed, despite his fortune of over 100 million nineteenth-century dollars. His son, William Henry Vanderbilt, alleged to be the richest man in the world at that time, continually haggled over the bills for his lunches ("I didn't *order* coffee last Tuesday"). John D. Rockefeller gave a groundskeeper a $5 Christmas bonus and then docked him $5 for spending the holiday with his family. And once when he thought he and his family had been charged for too many chickens at a restaurant he demanded that the plates be returned so he could count the bones.

A bank teller recently reported that a wealthy woman who makes deposits of several hundred thousand dollars every few days insists on the return of the paper clips with which she holds her checks together—a story that calls to mind such famous misers as Russell Sage, who haggled over the price of an apple when he had an income of $5 million a year, and bought all his clothes at fire sales. Or Kresge, who lined his shoes with paper and wouldn't have his clothes pressed for fear of wearing them out too soon. Or John D. Rockefeller, Jr., who inherited a billion dollars and refused ever to tip. Or Hetty Green, who once objected that a 10-cent bottle of medicine was too expensive, and when the druggist protested that it cost a nickel for the bottle alone promptly walked home and brought back her own bottle. When her son injured his knee Green got him some old clothes and tried to smuggle him into a charity ward to get free treatment (when this failed she refused to have him treated and he ultimately lost his leg).

The surprising thing is that this miserliness has to be discovered anew by journalists in each generation. A 1977 article in *Time,* for example, observed breathlessly that the new rich worked hard, lived modestly, and didn't race yachts or horses or become socialites or connoisseurs like their predecessors. *Time* was apparently comparing this century's moneymakers with the wives, children, and grandchildren of last century's moneymakers.

THE RINGWRAITHS

In J.R.R. Tolkien's fantasy *The Lord of the Rings,* there are nine great kings, possessors of rings of power. Over the years they are gradually devoured by the power they possess until they lose material substance altogether and are forced to borrow the physical bodies of other beings in order to make their way about. They are called the Ringwraiths.

Something quite similar often seems to happen to those who devote their lives to money. The money seems to eat them away, inside and out. Inside, they lose joy and spontaneity and generosity of impulse. Outside, they seem to wither, to become pale and drawn and fragile-looking.

It is difficult, of course, to decide how much of this is just the aging process. But certainly not all old men look as ravaged as Howard Hughes or as desiccated as Rockefeller or Mellon or Getty. In Pablo Picasso the fire burned in his eyes right up to his death. The withering of Heavy Addicts is extraordinary enough so that observers have felt compelled to comment upon it.

John D. Rockefeller, for example, although rather tight-lipped and suspicious-looking almost from birth, was quite solid in appearance until his mid-fifties, when he had consolidated his fortune. Suddenly he became stooped, lost all his hair (the result of a nervous disease called alopecia), and began to complain of fatigue, sleepless nights, and digestive ailments. The wispy, mummified look that we associate with his name only appeared after he became wealthy: "As his days were absorbed in the endless orchestration of his income and expenses, of investments and charities, of corporate strategy and legal defense, it became questionable whether he had mastered the money or the money had mastered him."

Andrew Mellon, possibly the wealthiest and certainly the most powerful of all the Heavy Addicts, looked like "a tired double-entry bookkeeper afraid of losing his job; worn, and tired, tired, tired." He was called "a wisp" and a "shadow of a man." Paul Getty even at sixty-seven gave "an impression of great physical fragility, which is increased by the almost unnatural pallor of his face."

The most dramatic example is Howard Hughes. As early as 1961 he was abnormally skinny and bedraggled-looking, and a few years later he was described as looking "like a witch's brother." In his last years he weighed only 90 pounds; "his body was starved, dehydrated, and atrophied to a pitiful skeleton resembling those of the victims of Dachau and Buchenwald." He had severe bedsores that had not healed for years— one so bad that his scapula was actually protruding from the flesh. His nails were an inch long and curling in. He suffered from anemia, arthritis, and constipation. (He once sat on the toilet for 72 straight hours—without enemas he would go as long as 28 days without a movement.) He died in a state of malnutrition and gross neglect, a prisoner in a jail of his own making. He had fifteen personal attendants that he paid well and controlled rigidly, yet a doctor who examined the body said he would have gotten better care had he been a skid row wino.

PLEASURE AND FRIENDSHIP

One reason for this evaporation of life's juices in the very rich is an increasing inability to take pleasure. Max Gunther observes that "the type of man most likely to grow very, very rich is the type of man least likely to enjoy it." Thorndike uses almost the same words: "many of those who acquire great wealth seem to be temperamentally the least likely to enjoy it." Rees' typical multimillionaire has "very little aptitude or instinct for pleasure." His personal life is "thin and brittle, even melancholy." The yachts of the rich lie empty (Onassis used the *Christina* about once a year); their magnificent paintings are "doomed to hang unseen" in some unvisited mansion (Getty, for example, was "a connoisseur who seldom sees his treasures"); they give huge parties but don't show up themselves. Howard Hughes always lived in the most expensive resorts but never took advantage of the pleasures they had to offer. Addicts never see the rainbow because they're too busy looking for the pot of gold.

A recent millionaire observed wryly that while people expect success and money to solve their problems, in fact it merely "throws the real problems into sharp relief. Like, why can't one sustain a relationship?" H. L. Hunt couldn't remember the name of the "only pal I ever had," and for most of the Heavy Addicts true friendship has been a luxury they felt unable to afford. Paul Getty's third wife called him "the most lonely person I've ever known. He wants to meet the other person but can't." (His difficulty seems less mysterious when we learn that on his first date with her he bought an expensive dinner and managed to stick her with the check.)

Max Gunther, generally an admirer of Addicts, observes that "self-made rich men often have a peculiar lack of warmth, an inability to form a close, lasting relationship with man, woman or child." Howard Hughes was so desperately lonely that he would call up Robert Maheu and talk for hours on the phone just for company. Yet he insisted on one-way communication—no one was allowed to phone him or even talk to him unless he initiated conversation.

Hughes was not nearly so unusual as we like to think: wealthy, paranoid, depressed recluses are a dime a dozen. The rich attract other Addicts and very quickly come to feel that no one cares for them—only for their money. This is likely to be at least partly true. Because of their wealth, genuine affection is in very short supply for Addicts and they therefore need very badly to control and coerce it. But the more they do, the less they can trust what they get. Money can be trusted, of course, but it doesn't satisfy the need. The more money, the less trust; the less trust, the more money; and so on, ad infinitum. Even their children cannot be trusted, for if they are at all like their parents—trusting only in money—they are waiting anxiously for them to die.

FOR THE CHILDREN

Many wealth addicts claim that the reason they are so agitated and driven in their personal lives is that they want security for their children. They justify the oppression and environmental destruction in which they engage on the grounds that people should be able to provide for their own. Since the health, happiness, and well-being of our nation are being jeopardized for the benefit of these children, let's see how our expensive investment is coming along.

Psychiatrists and social scientists who have studied the children of wealth addicts find them as a group to be unhappy and self-centered, with a poor sense of reality and an inability to form deep, stable contacts with others. Michael Stone and

Clarice Kestenbaum, for example, find that the most common symptoms of wealthy children are "chronic depression," "feelings of emptiness," and a "pervasive and long-lasting sense of sadness, ennui, and discouragement about the future." Roy Grinker, Jr., finds that the children of the wealthy tend to be "empty, bored, and chronically depressed," and often become "emotional zombies."

Robert Coles observes that since wealthy children are treated as if they were the center of the universe they tend ultimately to believe it. In the self-portraits of rich American children, for example, the figure of the child fills up the whole page, while in those of Hopi children the figure is merely a dot in a rich landscape. Children of wealth addicts tend to grow up with a sense of what Coles calls "entitlement"—a feeling that the world and its bounties belong to them by right. They assume that whatever they want will automatically be pleasing to everyone else. They lack the capacity for tenderness, according to Grinker, and their narcissism turns people away. Like Howard Hughes, they hate large groups because they can't control them—they fear people might jostle them or even ignore them completely.

Addicts like to complain that taxes and social programs take from the industrious and give to the idle. Yet while taxes do this occasionally, inheritance (which has sometimes been called a welfare program for the wealthy) does it inevitably. Andrew Carnegie said he "would as soon leave to my son a curse as the almighty dollar." But if many children respond to this curse by feeling entitled, others feel guilty and burdened by the money, and try to reduce their feeling of unworthiness by making more of it. They're born addicted, in other words, like the infant of an alcoholic mother—learning to tope as it nurses. Getty, Hughes, Mellon, the Rockefeller brothers— "most of the heirs to great fortunes, it seems, are busy making more money."

Coles found that many wealthy children are obsessed with a need to be perfect and are terrified of failing. They feel they're beginning life's struggle with a personal deficit and need to achieve a great deal just to live up to all the advantages they have inherited. Even when an Addict's child *does* achieve something it often seems a hollow victory, since "what might be a gamble for an ordinary man could easily become a sure thing when a Rockefeller exerted the force of his name, his connections, and his capital on it." One study of the very rich found that third-generation children rarely produced in their fields "anything really valuable or standing above the average level," a finding that brings to mind the remarks of William Vanderbilt: "My life . . . was laid out along lines which I could foresee almost from my earliest childhood. It has left me with nothing to hope for, with nothing definite to seek or strive for. Inherited wealth is a real handicap to happiness."

Whether the children of Addicts turn out "spoiled" or hyper-responsible they are dealing with the same handicap: a feeling that they are small and insignificant in relation to the huge pile of money. The "spoiled" ones react by inflating themselves—they see the money as part of them, making them larger than life, and assume that the rest of the world will naturally want to subordinate itself to their wishes. The "responsible" ones see themselves merely as part of the money, their role in life to serve and increase the family fortune. In this role they may behave with equal arrogance—indeed, the "spoiled" ones have undoubtedly done less harm in our society than the humble, responsible "caretakers."

There is, of course, a third solution: if the money keeps you from finding out who you are, get rid of the money. This is much easier to say than to do, however. Some of the fourth generation Rockefellers have struggled both to rid themselves of their money and to atone for it, but they have had to combat their own feelings of deprivation to do so: "Strangely enough," says Peggy Rockefeller, the daughter of David, "we had a sense of there not being enough to go around—not enough food, not enough love."

Roy Grinker argues that the "spoiled rich kids" he sees are

as deserving of his sympathy and psychiatric skills as other human beings. This is certainly true, but it can be misleading. All addicts of all kinds are deserving of our sympathy, because they believe themselves deficient and feel dependent on some kind of prop. But the first step toward finding one's inner resources is getting rid of the props. Sympathy that supports growth is important to people; sympathy that supports and fosters the addiction is hurtful and destructive. The best time to extend sympathy to the children of Addicts who have been injured by money is when the money is being discarded or removed.

PARENTAL DEPRIVATION AND COMPETITION

Not all the troubles of Addicts' children come from the money itself. Some are created by the fact that so many Addicts bring a coldness and an emptiness with them wherever they go, and this makes itself felt strongly within the family. Andrew Mellon's father, who built the foundations of the family fortune, was so cold as to be "hardly human."

H. L. Hunt "felt no passion for anything or anybody." He had three wives, with several children by each, and seems to have neglected all three families impartially. After he died they became embroiled in lawsuits, even though the children in all three families were provided with trust funds involving hundreds of millions of dollars. Trying to account for this strange behavior, one author suggested that "they seemed to feel as if a share of the estate was somehow equal to a share of their father's heart." Clearly, they had little else to go on: "Hunt's children could never be entirely certain of their father's affections for them. All they had left to look to was H. L.'s will."

One of the popular stereotypes about the children of Addicts is that although their parents may reject and ignore them, they may be brought up by loving servants and hence escape serious psychic crippling. This pleasant myth overlooks the competitiveness of the Addict: Grinker finds that servants are often fired when they get too close to a child, no matter how little interest in the child the parents themselves may have. And even if the Addict is fond of the child in his own way, the cold favor of a man like H. L. Hunt or Judge Thomas Mellon, while perhaps not a kiss of death, is certainly a kiss of ice. Andrew Mellon, for example, became his father's favorite at the age of nine when his older brother died, and began immediately to be groomed for a role in his father's bank. This interest, according to a cousin, "shortened A. W.'s boyhood." Like John D. Rockefeller, Jr., whom he resembled in some ways, he collapsed under the weight of his responsibilities in adolescence and had to leave school to recover.

Hunt's favorite son, "Hassie," who was often brought along on Hunt's oil explorations, had been "pressured to live up to H. L.'s standards ever since he was a small boy." Always subject to "fits of odd behavior" he was finally hospitalized at twenty-six and on his release "withdrew from the world almost completely." Hunt became convinced that lobotomy was the only solution and had one performed against the advice of everyone, including Hassie's doctors. Hunt once said he'd give up all his money to have Hassie recover, yet his daughter Margaret stated flatly: "My father destroyed Hassie."

Henry Ford loved his son, Edsel, whom he named after his best friend in childhood, yet, like Hunt, he couldn't seem to stop himself from dominating Edsel and crippling his growth. Like most Addicts, Ford wanted Edsel to be "a replica of himself." When Edsel became a capable executive, Ford decided he wasn't "tough" enough. He often countermanded his orders and even sent the infamous Harry Bennett to spy on and harass him, ostensibly to "develop his character." Edsel developed ulcers instead, and at the age of forty-nine died of cancer, "undoubtedly aggravated by the constant frustrations under which he had to live and work."

Most Heavy Addicts seem to have little ability to allow other living things to grow on their own. Ego-driven as they are, they have almost no sense of the world as a living fabric of which they are a part. They need to manipulate everything in a conscious, deliberate way. Since they can't share leadership or even ownership, it isn't too surprising that they have trouble allowing their own children a place in the sun. Ford wanted Edsel to be a "rugged individualist" like himself, who wouldn't be "pushed around," yet at the same time would carry out every one of his father's wishes. H. L. Hunt boasted of Hassie's oil-finding ability, yet was displeased when he made a huge oil strike on his own. In a way, leaving large sums of money to your children expresses this ambivalence, since it's a gift that enfeebles the children as it enriches them.

FEAR AND CONTROL

Fear is the most ruthless of all emotions. We talk of aggression and sexuality as if they were the most difficult to manage, but compared to fear they're barnyard animals. Pure sexuality is easily sated, pure anger soon discharged. Only when tinged with fear do they become twisted, violent, and unmanageable. Fear is the one emotion that shrinks from confrontation with its object, thus lending itself to the weaving of fantasies—from which escape is impossible. Any emotion, mood, feeling, or impulse that seems chronic and difficult to discharge is always alloyed with fear. And because it shrinks from confrontation with reality, fear is the source of all feelings of inner emptiness or lack or inadequacy, and hence, of all addiction.

Lamott remarks that robber barons like Astor, Gould, Sage, Morgan, Fisk, Rockefeller, and Vanderbilt were "emotional cripples, grown men governed by the fears that properly belong to an adolescent boy peering in the mirror for signs of a moustache." But Lamott doesn't go back far enough—most Addicts seem to operate at the prepubescent level, that age when little boys are hyperactive, play incessantly with guns and dream of military exploits. Howard Hughes preferred spy and adventure movies without women and would instruct his projectionists to "skip the mushy parts," just as a ten-year-old would. Most of the Heavy Addicts have been warm in their support of fascist political regimes—partly from their morbid fear of Communism but mostly from their general dread of "weakness." The mild-mannered Andrew Mellon, for example, was a great admirer of the absurd braggart Mussolini.

People are difficult to manage, and those who can't handle relationships often retreat to inanimate objects. Howard Hughes once remarked that science and mechanics interested him more than people, and Henry Ford, who developed the assembly line to give him the kind of control over workers that he had over machines, was "constitutionally . . . unable to relinquish or delegate authority."

Rockefeller was said to crave order "as the drunkard craves alcohol" and devoted much of his life to eliminating the "anarchy" of a comparatively free market. Even when he retired to his estate he often had his gardeners rearrange the trees, moving them around "as an interior decorator would move chairs." This antipathy to spontaneity, even in nature, affects many Addicts. William Randolph Hearst was also an inveterate tree-mover.

Such an extreme need for control betrays great inner fragility, and this is aggravated by the possession of money itself. When you use money to insulate yourself from risk and change, your adaptive capacity shrinks and atrophies. This is one reason why most Addicts can't stop making money: they sense this loss and seek still more money to counteract it. One Addict expressed this anxiety when he said that if he didn't remain active he would be in danger of "stagnating and becoming senile." The more you use something outside yourself to prop yourself up, the weaker you feel and the more propping up you need. This is also why Addicts so often have sexual problems: their sexual potency is heavily tied to how potent they feel financially. A severe market decline, according to a well-known brothel keeper, can produce an epidemic of impotence: "When the stock market goes up the cocks go up; when the stocks go down the cocks go down."

When the world got too complex for Howard Hughes he simply constructed his own narrow one in which he could make all the rules. "In the everyday world a recluse who cowers naked amid self-neglect in his bedroom is called insane," and probably less than a quarter of the patients in our mental hospitals (initially, at least) are as crazy as Hughes was. Most of them are there because they've become a nuisance to someone. Hughes was an extraordinary nuisance to all those around him (to the whole country in fact), but he could *pay* for being a nuisance, and he did, creating his own one-patient mental hospital with a large staff controlled, in large part, by the inmate.

Hughes was particularly concerned about controlling *input.* No one could call, talk, look, or touch without invitation. He had a terrible fear of being entered in any way. One expression of this was his germ phobia. Aides and typists had to wear white gloves and he went through constant rituals of decontamination. (Since the Ego doesn't like the idea that all life is interconnected, and refuses to acknowledge its own participation in that unity, all this living and stirring becomes a creeping invasion, an alien thing. Hence the intense fear Hughes and Getty had of "other people's" germs.) Yet, as Phelan points out, Hughes died by poisoning himself from within—a perfect example of the limitations of conscious, Ego control.

Hughes hated to acknowledge any interdependence. It bothered him that anyone who drilled a well and thereby tapped the water table was "in effect a neighbor." Like many Americans, Hughes thought freedom existed when everybody had his or her own cage. This fear of entanglement became overpowering because Hughes had lost the ability to meet anyone head on, on an equal basis. He "always cringed away from confrontations," using his power and money to pass the buck.

The Irving hoax pushed Hughes into the world again for a brief time, and Phelan observes that both his health and his spirits seemed to improve with the risk and stimulation that this caused. He was thrust into daylight, viewed by strangers, discussed in the news, forced to move about in public places without his "insulation"—the realization of all of his worst fears. Yet losing control over his environment seemed to bring him to life. He began to think of going into the world a bit more, which disturbed some of his aides, who might then lose their reason to exist. Ultimately, however, he relapsed back into his "normal" pattern and died.

This need for control may have been particularly extreme in Hughes but is conspicuous in most Addicts. Rees comments that the six Addicts he studied were most alike in the way they handled his interview with them. Like Hughes, they had trouble letting anyone else initiate things. They greeted his request with "reserve, suspicion, and hostility" and gave many reasons why the interview probably would not happen. Then, after a long delay, they would send a message saying they were available for a meeting at once. When the interviews began they became "passionately and almost pathetically anxious" that every trivial detail about their complex operations be correct. From elusive subjects they became "embarrassingly overenthusiastic collaborator[s]," who deluged the interviewer with information and were "extravagant" with their time.

These men obviously took themselves very seriously and wanted complete control over every detail of any process involving them. This is not a particularly unusual trait in our culture, especially in men. Yet it reveals an intense fear of meeting life on its own terms—of being vulnerable to experience.

A LIFE SENTENCE

Samuel Marquis once remarked that Henry Ford, who could arrange the parts of a car so skillfully, had no appreciation of the importance of balance in his own personality: "If only Henry Ford were properly assembled!" But what inspires such severe overcentralization in Addicts? A balanced personality grows in a balanced environment—given a variety of experiences and models, a child will naturally gravitate toward wholeness. But when a child's emotional eggs are crowded into one parental basket this natural tendency can easily be overwhelmed. A child with many friends and relatives, exposed constantly to assorted personalities and backgrounds, can find what it best needs out of that assortment. But the child whose happiness is for any reason primarily dependent on the love of one other person is ripe for overcentralization: the threatened loss of that love is a danger to which the Ego typically responds with heroic measures.

It isn't too surprising, then, that so many Addicts were lonely children with stern, ambitious mothers who were the centers of their lives and who demanded a great deal of them. Paul Getty's mother, for example, was a powerful woman who masterminded her husband's career and then "imposed her will" on Paul, particularly in the matter of thrift. She fought him bitterly and successfully for control of his father's company for many years; yet although he claimed he would have been a billionaire ten years earlier if she hadn't blocked his path, he never stopped seeking her approval. He claimed that "no one ever had a better mother" despite their bitter corporate struggles. Speaking of an important moment late in his career, he said: "I resolved to do my best to be worthy of Mama."

Henry Ford's mother also loomed large in his life; she taught him to read and trained him to feel that the right to play had to be earned—that duty came before one's own desires. She shamed him mercilessly whenever he departed from these values. A stern, hardworking woman, she believed in keeping busy so you didn't notice how tired you were. Like all procrastinating solutions, it eventually caught up with her and she died when Henry was only thirteen. He described the house after she died as "like a watch without a mainspring." Later he restored the house as a shrine to her memory—complete with her dresses, dishes, and other personal effects. Throughout his life he completely accepted her intense commitment to the work ethic and had absolutely no use for play or "idleness" of any kind, yet he devoted his entire career to the development of labor-saving techniques. He once said, "I have tried to live my life as my mother would have wished. . . . I believe I have done, as far as I could, just what she hoped for me." An uncle once told him he was "just like her."

John D. Rockefeller also worshipped his mother, who brought him up alone and taught him thrift. H. L. Hunt was educated almost entirely, and apparently quite extensively, by his mother. Cornelius Vanderbilt got his first stake, his love of money, and his miserliness from his mother. Andrew Carnegie's widowed mother lived with him until she died, and made him promise never to marry while she still lived. Howard Hughes's mother made "a full-time job" out of raising him: she worried constantly about his health, his isolation as an only child, and his "supersensitiveness." Her obsessive concern made her an "overpowering influence" in his life while she lived, and, indeed, ever afterward.

Examples can easily be multiplied, for an amazing number of Addicts were the focus of such stern maternal ambitions. These were women struggling with difficult and disappointing lives—women of energy and strength who had no legitimate outlet for it except to channel it into their sons, who, as a result, devoted their whole lives to a vain effort to please and satisfy them. For how can a vicarious victory be satisfying? (Now that women are finding their own avenues of self-assertion this particular form of neurosis may become less common.) Small wonder that other people so often found these men cold and distracted: most Addicts find others of interest only to the degree that they can help them in their lifelong struggle to fulfill their mothers' dreams.

Having all your emotional eggs in one basket gives you tremendous focus and concentration. Pursuing an unreachable goal gives you an overdeveloped will and an overpowering need for control. For people who drive and control others are always themselves driven: "The mental capacities of the success hunters I observed," says Edmund Bergler, "were those of a prisoner looking for escape."

5

The Ego Mafia and
the Addictive Economy

*Money attracts egotism
and irresistibly leads to its misuse.*
EINSTEIN

The tyranny of the Addict's Ego is reversible. The Ego is capable of growth and can be trained to become more democratic. The increasing emphasis in recent decades on feeling and spontaneity, on the body, on meditation and other spiritual disciplines, on altered states of consciousness, on paranormal faculties—all of these seek to bolster grass-roots democracy and make the Ego more responsive to its Constituents.

Unfortunately, however, Americans are so resolutely individualistic that they fail to realize this is not an individual matter, and their efforts at democratization are subverted. The desire to democratize the Ego is coopted by the Ego itself and twisted into new forms of despotism. "Feeling-fulness" becomes self-conscious catharsis. Spontaneity becomes hedonism, i.e., gifts of pleasure that the Ego doles out to its Constituents without ever for a moment relinquishing control. Spirituality becomes arrogance and meditation a withdrawal from the living world. And the exploration of altered states is perverted into the addictive quest for a constant high. The awareness of our interconnectedness is the keystone of all efforts at democratization, and in its absence the Ego will make a mockery of all such efforts and distort them beyond recognition.

Furthermore, despotic Egos do not act alone, in isolation. They meet continually with other Ego-despots to support and protect each other—a kind of Ego Mafia. The purpose of the Ego Mafia is to create a world in which Ego-despotism will thrive—in which our Egos can convince each other that they are not parasitically dependent on their Constituents. For Egos like to pretend they were self-created, and to make this easier they try to build a world that reminds them increasingly of themselves and decreasingly of their Constituents.

It is the Ego Mafia that constructs rectangular buildings—that replaces the curving, irregular shapes of the natural environment with straight lines and right angles. If you live in a box, it's a lot easier to believe that your whole being is coextensive with your Ego. The Ego likes straight lines because it is simple-minded. It likes either-or definitions because it is binary. It detests paradox and the idea of a transcendent unity. It fears subtle shadings. It loves sharp boundaries and the illusion of separateness and autonomy. The Ego is a "rugged individualist."

The automobile is a characteristic Ego Mafia product: a mechanical device, based on binary principles, that walls us off from nature. Travel normally heightens our awareness of the interdependence of all life, but today we can ride in a box that gives us an illusion (rapidly crumbling as oil becomes scarce) of complete autonomy as we move along. All sensory input is cut off except for a minimal amount of vision (anyone who has biked or walked along a familiar road knows how little we see of our surroundings when we travel by car). Even in a convertible we experience only a wind caused by our own motion (and perhaps a sound caused by our own radio): sensory input is merely *self*-input.

Bureaucracy is another Ego Mafia device, a mirror image of the Ego on a social level. Imagine a small village where the inhabitants have lived together all their lives without appointed leaders or hierarchy of any kind, making decisions by informal consensus; then imagine a military group taking over the village and setting up formal leaders and hierarchical levels and requiring that all communications go through "proper channels" and be in writing (the social equivalent of "conscious"): this will give you a pretty fair notion of the Ego's relation to its Constituents. Bureaucracy makes people feel that only their Egos matter—that their Constituents are entirely irrelevant to the business at hand.

Authority, status, hierarchy, class—all are Ego Mafia creations. They define the world in terms of "higher" and "lower," and place stronger value on "higher" than "lower." This helps make us feel that the head is somehow "better" than the rest of the body. It reinforces our detachment from the ground. We see the earth as dirty and somehow inferior, although in fact it not only sustains us but is richer, denser, more packed with smells and energy and life than anything "above" it.

The Ego Mafia tries to build a world in which the Ego will feel comfortable and powerful—a world without bodies, filled only with Egos. No animals, plants, bacteria, or insects—no "blooming, buzzing, confusion." No feelings, no moods, no colors, no relationships, no ambiguities, no changes. Above all, no mystery. The Ego Mafia seeks a world of simple, mechanical processes, a world in which Egos can quietly sort out threat from nonthreat without being distracted—a world in which agendas are made and adhered to.

We live now in a society created by the efforts of the Ego Mafia to achieve this ideal goal. The Ego's Constituents aren't too happy with it. They invent horrible fantasies of what it would be like to live in a world that was even closer to the

Ego's goals. But in the end they usually give in to the Ego because they need structure and direction and because the Ego has convinced them to be afraid. One of the main things that Egos do at Ego Mafia meetings (which includes almost all business meetings in almost all organizations, great and small) is reinforce each other's scare tactics. An Ego Mafia meeting is like a workshop for military junta leaders in "How to Muffle Dissent and Forestall Popular Uprisings," taught by example.

The shape of this page, the uniform letters, the uniform spacing of regular rows of print—all are designed to make your Ego feel at home and your Constituents feel as if you were in Alphaville: "Hello! This is direct Ego-to-Ego communication with rectangular Constituent-screening that virtually eliminates noise. Do you read me?" Small wonder that we so often fall asleep reading, particularly when the message is as purified as the medium (a straight line may be the *shortest* distance between two points but it's rarely the most rewarding): "Listen, if he's going to shut us out and have a private summit conference, what do you say we get together and pull the plug on him?"

And this, of course, is the great joke. It's *my* Ego, after all, and yours is yours. Neither one can do a thing without us. They're just servants that have gotten out of hand. "Servants of the people." When we create our horrible fantasies of an Ego-pure world, our Egos dutifully help us write them down and try to get them published so we'll be successful and not be afraid anymore. My Ego is helping to write *this* down. And although it may have been our Egos that sold us a bill of goods in the first place, it was we who bought it.

And we can unbuy it. We can train our Egos to be more flexible and restore them to their true roles as Secretaries of Defense. But our task is made more difficult by the Ego Mafia, which dominates our world and enables our Egos to reinforce each other. When religious gurus talk of solving the world's problems through "changing human consciousness," they seem to share a naive vision of a simple world in which each human organism struggles alone to democratize itself. But the Egos are not alone and the world is not simple. Every day the power position of each Ego is strengthened by the Ego Mafia and the world rendered more and more compatible with the Ego's grandiose fantasies of being self-conceived and bodiless. And less and less compatible with the needs of the total organism for wholeness, balance, adventure, passion, involvement, participation, and play.

Ultimately, of course, the Ego Mafia will lose, since its entire effort is directed toward the maintenance of a delusion. Our Constituents also act in concert (although we hate to acknowledge it) and if the tyranny is carried too far the Constituents will rebel—not in the sense of individual madness, but by pushing their Egos into collective self-destruction. As the Ego Mafia creates a more and more suffocating environment for its Constituents, those Constituents will demand more and more retaliation against that felt threat. The Ego Mafia, after all, is parasitic. It has no life of its own, but derives all its strength, energy, and the little wisdom it has from its Constituents, and is ultimately governed by their wishes.

One obvious scenario for Ego Mafia self-destruction is nuclear catastrophe. Each step along the way to such catastrophe would be completely rational in the Ego's terms: threat leading to counter-threat, advantage to counter-advantage, and overkill to counter-overkill. The Ego's rational processes are used to make the weapons and to devise systems of delivery. (Even our "fail-safe" systems are based on the Ego's binary, threat-obsessed mentality: two armed men, whose joint participation is necessary to launch, sit at each missile silo watching each other for the signs of madness that would justify instant execution.) Yet all this Ego-made "rationality" is in the service of creating a powder keg so massive and so volatile that the probability of disaster escalates geometrically with every passing decade. The Ego Mafia, even as it denies the existence of Constituents, faithfully serves the desire of those Constituents to free themselves from its increasingly suffocating bondage by blowing itself up.

I have painted the despotic Ego as a kind of villain, and indeed, if we look at fictional villains, from Satan to Saruman, we find they're little more than portraits of the human Ego in its most despotic form: scheming, careful, paranoid, overcontrolled and overcontrolling, arrogant, never content, and so on. But how can this be reconciled with the idea that the Ego gets all its motives and energy from its Constituents?

It has been said that people get the kind of government they deserve, and this holds true within the individual organism. Even the Ego's fear of being overthrown is motivated by its Constituents, who are afraid of having to face the world unprotected and unmasked. We want our Egos to keep us from stumbling, from making fools of ourselves, from getting hurt, from arousing dislike or ridicule in others—in short, from all those experiences that help people learn and develop. We want our Egos to figure it all out in advance so we can walk through the world protected and in safety.

But these are the very desires that breed dictators. Learning and growth are impossible without the risk of occasional pain and hurt. You don't learn to dance or ride a horse by reading manuals and scheming and anticipating every possible eventuality. You learn by making a fool of yourself and falling down. Ego-ridden organisms are obsessed with avoiding mistakes: they want the Ego to plan, calculate, and predict before doing anything. But pediatricians say that a toddler with no bruises on its body is overprotected. We learn to avoid major errors by making small ones and learning from them. An organism that takes risks doesn't need a dictatorial Ego—it can learn on its own, without having to send every little piece of information through Central Processing before acting.

Every "individual" is in reality just a nodal point in two larger systems. One is the Ego Mafia. The other is the whole fabric of organized living matter, which is continually evolving, balancing, and making subtle attunements among its parts. Being close to nature enhances our awareness of participating in this unity, which, for want of a better term, we might call the "fabric of life." Being in a city building enhances our awareness of participating in the Ego Mafia, which is a mechanical rather than organic unity and hence much less challenging to our sense of being a proud, if lonely, atom.

The Ego Mafia exists, in large part, to deemphasize our participation in the fabric of life. It likes to invent boundaries and pigeonholes—to classify and categorize and analyze and find any way it can to break up (in our minds, at least) this organic unity of living matter. And in doing this it increases the very fear we seek to quiet. This is the whole problem with fear: other passions spend themselves when we act on them, and diminish. But when we act on the basis of fear the fear increases. Whether we hide or placate or kill out of fear, the fear feeds on the respect we give it. The only way to get rid of fear is to confront the source of it, which fear itself tends to prevent.

Fear is the failure to recognize our participation in the fabric of life. Hence it is fear that creates the Ego Mafia. (The opposite of fear is love, which is a recognition and expression of that participation.) But the Ego Mafia enhances that fear still further by trying to convince us that we are alone, isolated, inadequate, and without resource—save for our Egos, who will protect us, hide our deficiencies from the world, and obtain goods from the world to fill our emptiness.

Many people have noted that our entire economy is based on convincing people that they are inadequate—that there is a hole in them that a product would fill. As I have pointed out, this is what addiction is: the feeling that something's missing inside, that I'm incomplete unless I add something that's "out there." But now we know what that feeling of emptiness or incompleteness comes from: *the source of all addiction is the Ego's feeling that it is missing something, and what it's missing is one of its own Constituents that it refuses to listen to.* What our fear hides from us is that *we are connected with all of life and can draw on the strength of all of that life within us.* To the average American, brainwashed into individualism, that statement may seem like gibberish, but to many peoples of the world it contains no mystery at all.

In other words, the reason we keep looking outside ourselves for ways to fill our inner deficiencies is that the Ego is unaware of the rich talents of its Constituents. But the reason it sees its Constituents as deficient is that it will not accept the fact that in a fundamental sense all Constituents are one—that all organisms have common creative resources on which to draw. This is a hard nut for our Western minds to crack. Another way of saying it is that our so-called deficiencies are not *lacks* but *imbalances.* If, for example, a controlled man feels he lacks joy, the joy isn't *absent* from his being; it has merely been squeezed into a closet by the distended bulk of his excessive self-control. And, conversely, when a fun-loving man feels he lacks self-control, the control isn't absent but merely stifled by his desire to pursue every impulse. Convincing ourselves that we are actually *missing* these necessary traits saves us all the trouble of rearranging our internal furniture so that these stifled parts of ourselves can breathe and expand. What we take in, in fact, by way of addiction, usually helps keep the stifled traits exactly where they are. Alcohol, for example, may instill a temporary false confidence but continually shrinks real self-respect. In the same way, money suffocates feelings of *inner* security. The Ego of the addict is a little like Henry Ford, who fired his most creative managers and engineers and then complained that he had to do everything himself.

This reluctance to look at our problems as imbalances affects our attitudes toward disease. If we become ill, we don't like to think of it as a result of poor inner arrangement. We like to think that something (a "germ") has gotten into us that "doesn't belong" (despite the fact that we carry billions of them in our bodies at all times). Since the Ego likes to see itself as a lonely captain at the helm of a beleaguered ship of state, it tries to pass off any malfunctions in the organism as the result not of the Ego's own authoritarian and overcentralized rule, but of "outside agitators." This perpetuates the Ego's role as vigilant guardian by creating a definition of healing that is essentially military. The healer in our society is cast as a kindly policeman who cures the sick by hunting down these outside agitators and killing them.

Thus was born the germ theory of disease. Instead of seeing an organism as warped or out of balance, we see it as being invaded by dangerous aliens whose presence justifies military intervention by the healer. Heavy weapons are employed, in the form of drugs, surgery, radiation, "magic bullets," and so on. Even where no germ or virus can be found, as in heart disease, cancer, diabetes, mental illness, and the other major ailments of modern society, the attack model is employed anyway. We "fight" birth defects, "make war" on cancer, and seek to "wipe out" heart disease.

The Ego Mafia's preference for the germ theory is tied to its obsession with rigid boundaries and property lines. In nature boundaries are fluid, fuzzy, or nonexistent. It is the Ego Mafia that invents lines of demarcation (this is wrist, that is arm; this is foothill, that is mountain; this is biology, that is chemistry; this oxygen is your oxygen, that oxygen is my oxygen; these germs are your germs, those germs are my germs)—ignoring the fact that organic and inorganic matter, information, and live organisms are flowing in and out of us every second of our lives; that millions of cells are dying and being replenished each day and that the only thing physically constant about us through our lives is the rough approximation of a shape (and even that changes drastically). The human personality is a pattern developed in response to others: even its most rigid and unchanging postures are merely policies, dictated by the

Ego in response to someone's behavior in the dim past, however irrelevant and forgotten.

As a society, we also cling to illusions of separateness. Instead of looking at the imbalances within our own social and political system we spent decades fighting against the threat of Communism. The Ego Mafia continually fills our lives with misery and frustration which it then attempts to blame on external sources. Most of the cancer in the United States, for example, is caused by our own industrial products and by-products: pollution, radioactivity, food additives, drugs, pesticides, and so on. Cancer, in other words, is caused by our national commitment to help wealth addicts get rich. Yet countless millions have been spent in medical research trying to find a *virus* that could be linked to cancer.

The Ego Mafia exists to help despotic Egos short-circuit the fabric of life. Money is a great help in carrying out this function, since it reduces all that living complexity and variety to a single quantitative standard. Moneythink is the native language of the Ego Mafia.

But since Moneythink cuts off our awareness of our bonds with the fabric of life it creates a feeling of internal incompleteness, laying the foundation for an addictive society. In such a society the Addict feels himself to be normal. "After all," he argues, "everybody wants money" (those who don't are obvious lunatics and don't count). "Without money, how would you motivate people?" If we take the word "people" to mean everybody (since "everybody wants money"), then the question can be rephrased like this: "Without money, how would we get ourselves to do the work we want done?"

But with this phrasing the whole illusion crumbles. People are constantly doing work they want done without paying themselves for it. They work on their homes, they make things, they do volunteer work for the community. Scott Burns points out that if all the work Americans do "for nothing" were paid for at a minimum hourly wage, the total would be greater than the total of all wages and salaries paid out in the United States. Not only do Americans do more work without pay than they do *with* pay, but what they do is probably, on balance, better done, more useful, and less destructive than what they get paid for doing.

Obviously, we don't need money to get us to do what we *want* done. We simply do it. Money becomes necessary only to get us to do what we *don't* want done. Who would manufacture the useless junk that clutters our lives if they weren't getting paid for it? Once money exists, of course, it becomes another motive among many, and will compete with other motives. At that point many of the things we want done will be neglected in favor of activities that provide money. For example, we may not want to take the time to enrich and beautify and protect our environment because we are paying ourselves to destroy it.

The real problem with money as a motivator is that it tends to distort all activities—to twist them away from their original function of providing ourselves with needed goods and services. Since World War II, for example, we have fallen behind European societies in many of the ways that help define a country as "civilized" or "advanced." "In some categories, such as infant mortality [where we ranked twentieth in 1975], the United States is practically a developing country." Yet during this same period we have seen a whole crop of new Major Addicts emerge: the most recent large fortunes have been made in such enterprises as pet foods, deodorants, fast foods, cosmetics, cameras, breakfast foods, executive jets, boats and various other luxury items, or from stock manipulation and the building of conglomerates. Obviously, none of these enterprises provides essential goods or services for the people of our country. Yet while these fortunes were being made, the cost of food, clothing, housing, education, heat, and medical care climbed beyond the reach of large segments of the population. In 1976, to take just one example, there were over a million households with elderly people living on less than $2,000 a year, spending over half of their income on winter fuel.

Whenever money is used as a motivator the activity it motivates becomes redefined in terms of what will induce people to part with their money most easily. Food is grown and distributed not so as to provide the optimum nourishment for the greatest number of people, but so as to achieve maximum sales at minimum cost. Indeed, the original function of nourishing the populace has gone so badly awry that the populace is actually being poisoned.

The same absurdities can be found in the field of energy: it has been claimed that at least two hundred elderly people died during the winters of 1977 and 1978 because utilities shut off their heat. Meanwhile, at the same time that we were being pressured into a hasty acceptance of nuclear reactors because of an alleged scarcity of power, industrial users were still being given reduced rates that encouraged them to waste enormous amounts of electricity. With money as a motivator it becomes "cheaper" to have every high-rise in a city brilliantly aglow all night than pay a currently unemployed and hungry human being wages to turn the lights off. If corporations paid for their energy what the rest of us pay, they would learn very quickly to conserve to the point where nuclear power would become unnecessary. In 1978 a House measure designed to bring about such reform was killed by the Senate in response to furious utility lobbying.

We have come to expect such distortions in every field of endeavor: planned obsolescence and poor quality in manufacturing; showmanship, posturing, and "school"-founding in place of talent in the arts; athletes who are drugged and forced to play with injuries; college professors who avoid teaching so they can enhance their reputations, and hence income, through "research."

Medicine is the classic example of the distorting effect of money. While one function of a doctor is to save lives, studies have found that "the fewer the physicians in a population, the lower the mortality rate." Furthermore, "during physician strikes in Canada, the United States, England, and Israel, the death rate actually fell." Commenting on one such strike in Los Angeles a columnist suggested that the sharp decrease in the death rate was due to the marked reduction in surgical operations. A congressional subcommittee estimated that in the year 1974 alone, 2.4 *million* unnecessary surgeries were performed at a cost of *$4 billion* and leading to 11,900 deaths. Cancer surgery, for example, "does not appreciably prolong lives." Radical mastectomies, routine in this country for breast cancer, "have no higher cure rate than the 'lumpectomies' that are routine in England." A surgeon, asked why he nevertheless performed them, replied: "A radical mastectomy goes for $750. A simple mastectomy for $250. Which do you think we're going to say is best?" Perhaps this says all that needs to be said about the role of money in motivating people to perform socially useful tasks.

Americans believe that dangling money in front of people makes them work harder and become more efficient. It is true that some people will work harder for a monetary reward. The catch is that they aren't working to perform the task; *they're working to get the money and will distort their performance in any way possible* to get it. The lure of money may have made the surgeon quoted above willing and able to perform more and more mastectomies and to get good at it, and from an extremely narrow and shortsighted viewpoint this could be considered "efficiency." But if health is the goal, the money approach is not only "inefficient," it's a total failure. Nor is this an isolated or unusual example. Doctors themselves have estimated that anywhere from 50 percent to 85 percent of all illness in the United States is iatrogenic—that is, caused by medical treatment itself, particularly prescription drugs.

We talk about "motivating people" as if these "people" were not ourselves. We imagine some dimwit happily shoveling garbage under a cartoon balloon with a dollar sign in it. But that dimwit is *us*. We use money to push *ourselves* around. This approach, in which the right hand tries to manipulate the left, is an infallible sign of Ego Mafia domination. It's the same kind of thinking that funds research projects to find out how much radiation human beings can "tolerate" without getting leukemia, or how many food additives they can absorb without getting stomach cancer. It's the kind of thinking that allows some people to see their bodies as slaves to manipulate so as to get the most possible work out of them.

If work hasn't enough personal and social value in and of itself for us to perform it without money, then money won't persuade us to do it effectively. What it *will* do is motivate us to find ways to maximize the money we get for whatever work we *do* do. Getting people to chase money, in other words, produces nothing except people chasing money. Using money as a motivator leads to a progressive degradation in the quality of everything produced. We can see this everywhere around us. In fifty years the quality of everything we manufacture has steadily declined, along with all services. We treat this as a "given"—an obvious commonplace of modern life and "progress," as indeed it is.

Without greed as a motivator, we would still need food, houses, clothing, transportation, communications, health care, education, and so on. Do we imagine that without greed we would all lie down and starve? If so, we would be the first people in the history of the species to be so hopelessly addicted. In fact, all of us frequently work without compensation. I find myself that there is no difference in spirit between work I do that I get paid for and work I do that I don't get paid for, partly because I've made it a rule in my life that I will no longer do anything for money that I wouldn't be willing to do without compensation if I already had enough to live on. Most of what I've done for money in the last decade has been based on ability to pay, and while I can notice differences in my level of enthusiasm in providing these services, it never has to do with the amount of money offered, but rather with my perception of the sacrifice being made. I might devote very little energy to a talk given at a major university for less than my usual fee, for example, but I give everything I have when I agree to talk to a small, poor, and private group for a tenth or even a sixtieth of that fee. Work not done for money might be done more slowly, but it would also be done more truly, purposefully, and surely.

Our national practice of encouraging wealth addiction is often defended on the grounds that many things otherwise impossible can be accomplished with large concentrations of capital. But, as I said earlier, there are many ways to pool our resources without creating billionaires: taxes, pension funds, stocks, bonds. The only thing we achieve by encouraging wealth addiction is to place that concentrated wealth in the hands of those who are most severely addicted. Now this certainly speeds up decision-making. Actions can be taken on the merest whim without being hampered by annoying consideration of their long-range consequences. Americans have always felt that it was a God-given right for fools to be able to rush into any enterprise they liked without having to trouble themselves over its effects on others.

I am not opposed to letting things adjust themselves by having people butt their heads against each other, *provided people are more or less equal in power.* But as things stand, it's the Addicts who get to rush in without having to trouble themselves about whether the way they make money injures us, and it's the rest of us who get to be injured. And when the government makes half-hearted efforts to force Addicts to consider the effects of their greed on the people, they usually find massive support among Closet Addicts who dream of being in their shoes someday and echo their complaints of "overregulation."

Addicts are much too driven to be a safe repository for such decision-making power. Their needs are too frantic to allow thoughtful consideration of long-range consequences or side-effects. They are merely irritated when people raise questions about lead, asbestos, or pesticide poisoning, or the high death rate near airports, or the still unsolved problem of nuclear wastes and abandoned reactors, or the rapid and permanent destruction of the Amazon jungle (which produces half of the world's plant-generated oxygen and contains a third of the world's forested land), or the equally rapid loss of precious agricultural land through real estate development, destructive farming methods, and reckless irrigation techniques.

The formation of billionaires has another unfortunate side effect: the overwhelming influence of wealth addicts on elected officials. In the 1978 Senate races 85 percent were won by the biggest spenders. Addicts love to insist on legislators being paid far less than their responsibility merits: it makes them all the more accessible to subtle and unsubtle forms of bribery. The degree of control that Addicts have in Congress can be seen at a glance by looking at what they have made of the originally progressive income tax. Addicts also have a profound effect on foreign policy: Collier and Horowitz document, for example, the strong influence exercised by the Rockefeller family since World War II: Nelson was repeatedly successful in intensifying the Cold War—once successfully sabotaging a serious Soviet attempt at détente; David helped bolster the South African government when its repressive actions and massacres of blacks had thrown doubt on its viability; and the Vietnam War build-up was a "point-by-point implementation" of recommendations made by the Rockefeller brothers.

Using money as a motivator means that all activities in the society are dominated by the Ego Mafia and become increasingly divorced from the real needs of living beings. The society as a whole and the economy in particular become overcentralized and unbalanced. Greed becomes the driving force not merely for a few neurotic individuals, but also for the majority of the population, and when this happens—when greed is democratized—the entire economy becomes deranged, as we shall see in the next chapter.

6

The Democratization of Greed

Most Americans today think of themselves as just fighting for economic survival. Is this wealth addiction? Are all Americans potential Addicts? If not, why do we dedicate so much of our national energy to supporting Addicts? It has been estimated that the richest American of any era has controlled a sum of money equal to the annual wages of 100,000 skilled workers. How can we account for such extraordinary inequality? What do we mean when we say a Howard Hughes is "worth" as much as 100,000 productive men and women?

Usually such inequality is attributed to sheer power: those who control the means of production tend to control the government, armed forces, police, courts, news media, and so on. Yet there have been periods in history when the poor and powerless majority have overwhelmed the rich and powerful few. What makes the difference? What makes it possible for the greedy to impose their will on the less greedy?

Often we find the moderately poor in America feeling so threatened that they are quite willing to step on the faces of

131

those less fortunate than themselves to avoid joining their ranks. Yet rarely do they question the motives and behavior of those wealthier than they. Why is this so? Some kind of tacit collusion on the part of a large part of the population seems to maintain the power position of the Addict.

A Senate committee in 1974 found that the wealthiest 1 percent of our population owns *eight* times as much as the poorer *half* of our population. According to Lundberg, two-thirds of all investment assets in the United States are held by 3 percent of the population. Furthermore, this disparity between rich and poor has increased over the last two decades, partly because, as many writers have pointed out, the poor pay more. They pay more, first, because they are economically powerless—forced always by their lack of economic resources to buy in a seller's market and sell in a buyer's market. Only the affluent are in a position to take advantage of real bargains. The poor pay more, second, because they are ignorant and can easily be manipulated into making bad investments. It was largely poor and middle-class people, for example—duped by patriotism—who bought Series E Savings Bonds at a rate of interest no rich person would ever consider. And it is the poor who put any surplus money they have in savings accounts where the interest rates are lower than the rate of inflation. (Thus, while the depositors are actually losing money by lending it to the banks, the banks are in effect getting interest-free loans which they use to lend money back to other poor people, through installment buying, at 18 percent interest.) Finally, the poor pay more because they are politically unorganized and less able to protect themselves from discriminatory legislation, especially tax laws.

Of the income tax breaks available to individuals, all but a tiny fraction go to those earning more than $20,000 a year, although these make up only a quarter of those who file. Between 1971 and 1976 Congress wrote eighty-six tax breaks into law, many of them without testimony from a single witness and the rest supported mainly by those who derived direct financial benefit. In that period more than $161 *billion* was lost to federal revenues "without a single publicly recorded vote by Congress or by its tax-writing committees." In the last fiscal year tax breaks cost the government $136 *billion.* This kind of welfare for the rich is much costlier than welfare for the poor. One economist has calculated that if all such tax loopholes were plugged, tax rates could be cut by 45 percent. As Lamott points out, it is the rest of us who create the great fortunes of the wealthy: "Each dollar that Getty or Hunt is permitted to keep by grace of the depletion allowance must be paid into the treasury by a machinist or a high school teacher. . . ." Americans are reluctant to recognize this because of our national commitment to individualism—the delusion that what one person does has no effect on anyone else.

Furthermore, tax advantages for the wealthy have sharply increased during the past twenty-five years. The graduated income tax was supposed to "soak the rich," and did to an extent for the first few decades of its existence. In the 1930s *two-thirds* of the federal income tax revenue came from people earning over $100,000, but by the 1960s over half came from people earning less than $10,000. The capital gains tax—of benefit to few besides the wealthy—has been cut twice; and in the early 1960s the maximum income tax was cut from 91 percent to 70 percent—a move obviously of benefit only to millionaires, few of whom pay anywhere near that amount in any case. Lamott suggests that most Addicts pay about 30 percent to 40 percent, while many pay less than 1 percent. According to an IRS official, furthermore, a higher and higher proportion of the tax burden has fallen on individuals, while the corporate tax share has consistently diminished over the years. To give some indication of how extreme this can be, an oil company in 1951 with a net income of about $4.5 million paid less income tax than a married couple with three children and an income of $5,600. How does it happen, then, that the resentment of taxpayers has always fallen, not upon the wealthy or on the corporations they control, but upon governments, deprived of reasonable revenues, and on the poor?

One reason why Addicts have been spared this resentment is the widespread acceptance of the "trickle-down" theory of wealth, which argues that if we give all our money and resources to Addicts, they will use it in ways that will bring prosperity to all. Corporations like to boast of how many jobs they "provide," but they strive continually to reduce this number and "cut labor costs," thus minimizing the trickle. Prices are rarely rolled back when costs drop, yet increases are automatically passed on to the consumer. This is hardly startling, since corporations exist to make profits, and those profits must be extracted from either workers or consumers.

If money were purely a medium of exchange, it would tend to distribute itself rather evenly, like water, since nothing inherently belongs to anyone, and what one person can produce alone is only somewhat more or less useful than what anyone else can produce alone. But, as we have seen, wealth addiction is like a valve that allows money to flow only one way—toward those who already have it: as money flows about in a continuous circle, the "haves" skim a little off the top in each exchange. If all economic exchanges were completely fair, differences in wealth would obviously be small and temporary. The existence of large and chronic differences is a clear indication that swindling has occurred in the exchange process. The degree of inequality is a measure of the extent of the swindle.

The paradox in this is that the entire economic system depends on trust—a basic shared belief that economic transactions *will* be fair. The belief of the "have-nots" that the system is fair thus not only sustains the system but also makes it possible for the "haves" to cheat them, since the "haves" can skim only if there are enough "have-nots" with enough faith in the system to be skimmed. The chronic inflation we experience now represents the beginning of a breakdown of this willingness to support an exploitative system, a point I'll discuss later in this chapter.

I suggested that wealth addiction creates a valve that opens to let money flow toward the rich and closes to prevent it flowing toward the poor. Obviously the valve doesn't work perfectly or the poor would soon have nothing at all, money would stop circulating, the economic system would break down altogether, and money would be worthless. At times this has come close to happening, but usually the valve is leaky enough to keep things going. Indeed, the valve must be *made* to leak in order that exploitation doesn't reach the point where it destroys the system altogether. A perfect valve would kill the goose that lays the golden egg.

But how many leaks are to be allowed in the valve, and where are they to be placed? All the "haves" want to have the holes punched in someone else's backyard. A hole punched in the valve makes the system work more fairly, but everyone wants that fairness introduced somewhere far from home. Hence hole punching is always worked out in the realm of politics. Most political struggle revolves around (1) getting holes punched, (2) deciding where they are to be punched, and (3) finding ways to quietly plug them again without anyone noticing.

Hole punching usually occurs in short bursts, after a long period of unusually extreme exploitation. The implementation of the income tax under Wilson was one of these, the New Deal another. Since World War II there have been no major holes punched in the money valve, despite a few pinpricks during the Johnson administration. Efforts made to channel money toward the poor have foundered because the valve itself has been left intact. Thus a flow of money has several times been initiated, but never reached its purported destination.

There is a Washington cliché that "you can't solve a problem by throwing money at it," and if your "problem" involves any attempt to reduce inequality the statement is quite true.

This is because of what I call the Poultry Principle. Anyone who has ever distributed feed to a group of domesticated chickens, ducks, or geese is probably aware of the near impossibility of getting any of it past the greedy ones to the less gluttonous. Wherever you throw it, the greedy chickens are there. In other words, "throwing money" at a problem simply brings all the wealth addicts out of the woodwork (mixing our metaphors a bit) to gobble it up. A good example of this was the New Deal farm program, ostensibly intended to help poor farmers withstand the economic power of suppliers, distributors, and banks. Instead, it created agribusiness, crushing the small farmer and making rich corporations richer. The trouble with "handouts to the poor" is that they tend to be intercepted by middle-class hands, which are larger and better suited to grasping. Medicaid and Medicare, to take another example, have done a very poor job of bringing health care to the poor, but a very good job of enriching doctors. In the first year doctors' fees rose two and one-half times as fast as the cost of living, while a third of all Americans living below the poverty level remained unaffected.

Private attempts to punch holes in the money valve are no more successful. Medical charities subsidize doctors and research scientists seeking to enhance their professional reputations within their fields, and all charities subsidize middle-class fund-raisers and publicists. Even charities designed specifically to help the poor and hungry rarely pass more than a fraction of their collected funds to the needy themselves— sometimes less than 5 percent. This isn't to be wondered at— no significant reduction in the world's hunger and poverty will occur until greed and power-lust can themselves be made unprofitable.

Since 1945, for example, hundreds of billions of dollars have been given to developing nations under the foreign aid program. Supposedly designed to make these nations economically independent, they have had exactly the opposite effect, leaving them helplessly in debt, destructively tied to the international economy, diverted from their own natural pathways toward healthful growth. Far from addressing themselves to the real social and economic problems of these countries, our aid programs have been largely subsidies for American manufacturers and technicians, who flooded developing areas with unsuitable techniques and equipment and created ripe conditions for exploitation by multinational corporations seeking cheap, unorganized labor and new markets. As Ramón Margalef observes, exploitation reduces maturity—the more mature system draining off the energy the less mature system would normally use to mature on its own. This is done by reducing diversity in the less mature system, for "pumping more energy in and out of a system simplifies it." In Third World countries this often takes the form of homogenizing agricultural production—raising single cash crops on a mass scale—which increases dependence on heavy Western equipment, imported technicians, and fluctuations in international markets. Instead of feeding their own poor, building on their own diversity, and developing their own skills, these nations become powerless cogs in a larger system that exploits them as vigorously as it can. It's not an easy matter to punch holes in the money valve.

Our society is founded on the tension between two contradictory beliefs: (1) that human beings should be equal in opportunity and before the law, living in safety and freedom from exploitation, and (2) that our natural and human resources will be most effectively utilized if they are organized to serve wealth addiction. This tension is seen most dramatically in criminal law, where the fiction of equality must continually confront the reality of a double standard of justice for rich and poor.

When we examine this double standard closely, it seems to be based on an assumption—shared by judges and laypeople alike—that crime, especially larceny, is inherently working class. Middle-class people, therefore, are not "criminal types" by definition and should hence be treated differently. In 1978, for example, a jury that had convicted a thirty-year-old man of kidnap and robbery appended a plea of leniency, apparently on the grounds that he was heir to a $300,000 estate. The judge agreed, saying that the defendant was "not the typical crook we get in Superior Court." The idea seems to be that if a man doesn't *need* to steal in order to survive, he shouldn't be punished for it. This view reflects the fact that blue-collar crime is a hole in the money valve—it helps to equalize wealth again. The legal system serves in part to plug that hole. Since white-collar crime has nothing to do with equalizing wealth it is always treated leniently.

Since this system violates our most fundamental beliefs about democracy, a flagrant case may attract some grumbles —a Nixon, or a corporation that steals millions from the public and receives a $5,000 slap on the wrist. Yet most people seem to feel that the merest hint of public shame for a middle-class person is equivalent to ten years behind bars for a working man. Many thought Nixon had been "punished enough" by having to resign and accept a huge government pension. The same leniency was demanded for Prince Bernhard of the Netherlands, who admitted to taking over a million dollars in bribes, and was punished by having to feel very bad about it in public.

People are not unaware of the double standard. When two of H. L. Hunt's sons escaped conviction on a charge of obstructing justice, one of the sons remarked that "if Herbert and I had been just ordinary people, we could have been in real trouble." What people are unaware of is the depth of their class bias. This appeared dramatically in a California case where a doctor was convicted of eighteen counts of Medi-Cal and Medicare fraud. The Superior Court judge, who routinely sentenced poor people to prison for petty shoplifting, refused to imprison the doctor, giving him five years probation on the condition that he provide medical services on an Indian reservation. Both the district attorney and the public defender's office expressed outrage at the light sentence, especially when it was later discovered that the doctor was to receive a salary of $30,000 a year while serving this "sentence." It was clear that the judge found it impossible to treat as a criminal someone he might have played golf with.

In this the judge was not unique. The entire system of bail—as many people have pointed out—fosters this double standard. Poor people who cannot raise bail are forced to serve sentences of many months before they are brought to trial, even though in theory they are still innocent. Judges usually aggravate this inequity by arbitrary and punitive bail setting (a five-figure bail for a welfare recipient charged with streetwalking, for example—more than large corporations are often fined for polluting a whole river or poisoning consumers). Since prisons are usually more livable than jails, the punishment for being poor is far worse than the punishment for being guilty. Furthermore, judges and jurors are profoundly influenced by the current status of a defendant: those coming from jail are convicted twice as often as those out on bail.

Money thus confers respectability and hence innocence in the eyes of the law. Old battered cars are stopped by police far more often than new expensive ones, and expensively dressed persons are seldom harassed. To most of us crime is a disorderly, physical thing, and the thefts of the poor are obvious: they grab your purse or wallet or come in your house and take things. But the thefts of the rich are noiseless and unobtrusive. The rich steal from us when they bribe clients or suppliers or government officials and add the cost to the price of their products. They steal from us when their tax accountants find loopholes and again when they bribe Congress to create new ones. They steal from us when they collude to fix prices. They steal from us when they pollute our air and water and again when our tax dollars are used to clean it up and again when they take out full page ads to mislead us and again when they deduct those ads as a business expense. Most Americans feel that the rich man who hires a killer is less "criminal" than the man who pulls the trigger.

People argue that the crimes of the rich go unpunished simply because they have more power. But power is like money, it exists only as long as people believe in it. Nixon once boasted to a senator that "at any moment I could go into the next room, push a button and twenty minutes later sixty million people would be dead." Yet this power evaporated overnight. One moment everyone believed him to be the center of power, and that their own power would be enhanced by getting close to him. The next moment they all believed that it depended on getting as far away from him as they possibly could. The same thing can be seen in the Politburo or on the boards of large corporations.

Ultimately, power rests on public opinion—a fact that is easily forgotten because public opinion is so easily manipulated, so servile, so hungry for order. With all their power to bribe and coerce, Addicts could not flout the law as consistently and successfully as they do if the mass of the public did not in some way support them. And given a choice between blaming the rich for their problems or blaming the poor, the mass of the population will blame the poor every time.

THE CLOSET ADDICT

The 1978 tax revolt, for example, seemed to be based on the assumption that inflation and other economic problems were caused by government spending. Now, governments spend money on the poor, in welfare benefits and other services, and on the rich in graft, padded contracts, subsidies, and lost revenues through tax loopholes. Yet the wrath of the people fell only on the poor. When California passed its Proposition 13, billions of dollars in tax revenues were lost. Public services—libraries, schools, colleges, health services, etc.—had to be drastically cut. Far from making government more efficient, it caused a mass exodus among those public servants competent enough to find more secure and better-paying jobs in private industry. Large corporations benefited in other ways: the new law brought a $4 billion windfall in tax savings, very little of which was passed on to consumers. Indeed, since most of the largest beneficiaries were national or international corporations, much of the money simply left the state altogether. The net result of the "tax revolt" was the further impoverishment of the majority of voters.

The financial problems of New York City were also blamed on the poor, and on the "generosity" of the city to its indigent inhabitants. No responsibility was assigned to corporations who moved their plants out of the city in search of exploitable nonunion labor, leaving hundreds of thousands of workers on the city's unemployment rolls. These "runaway shops" often move to Third World countries where their substantial cost savings are passed on neither to local populations nor to American consumers. "Runaway shops pay skimpy wages overseas, but still charge the same prices for their products as when they were made in the United States." This is the money valve in action, skimming the poor at both ends.

It is easy for a large corporation to manipulate public sentiment about problems that are this complex. It is harder to understand public indifference to corporate violations of health, safety, and pollution laws. Almost every day we read of some corporation having knowingly exposed the public to lethal chemicals or radioactivity—dumping dangerous wastes, selling harmful medicines, putting toxic additives in our food. (Tax dollars support a huge laboratory in Arkansas whose purpose is "to find out just how many cancer-producing chemicals we could 'safely' consume.") Yet when these facts are exposed the outcry is not against those who profit from our ill health but against those who bring the facts to light. People joke that "everything in the world is carcinogenic" as if efforts to protect them against corporate murder were an annoying intrusion. How does this happen? Why do we applaud when wealthy corporations dine lavishly at our expense and then accuse the government of being a spendthrift when it has to pick up the check?

Corporations often try to excuse their acts by saying that they only serve their stockholders, implying all the while that these stockholders are a cross section of the general public. But Lundberg points out that less than 2 percent of the population owns 80 percent of all stocks (as well as 100 percent of state and local bonds and almost 90 percent of corporate bonds). It is primarily wealth addicts who profit from pollution and cancer.

Another example of misdirected blame is the Bakke decision, hailed as a victory against "reverse discrimination." White middle-class students were indignant that minorities with poorer grades were being admitted to schools that had turned the whites down. Yet, as one official pointed out: "While the middle class and the minorities are fighting it out . . . nobody seems to notice that the rich are still being assured of their quota." Bakke himself would have been admitted without having to go to court had not "at least five other less qualified white applicants been accepted ahead of him because of family clout." The key to getting into private schools is having a parent who will make a large contribution. At one school more than three-fourths of the accepted applicants had parents who made large financial contributions. (Yet many of these applicants were later awarded federal scholarships and loans as "needy students.") Anyone who has taught at an Ivy League school is familiar with the "Gentleman C student," and indeed, despite some superficial verbal facility, there are depths of stupidity in these schools not to be found in any other stratum of society, however impoverished. Officials at Harvard admitted during the late 1950s that 40 percent of their private-school applicants were admitted only because they came from "good" (i.e., rich) families who might leave bequests. *These* quotas, which probably kept close to a thousand bright public school students from being admitted to Harvard each year, produced no Bakke case, no outcry, no nothing.

Why are the rich immune from the anger so often directed against the poor for doing in a small way what the rich do on a grand scale? Is it the power of the rich to confer or withhold financial benefits? There is a widespread myth that the generosity of multimillionaires is all that stands between us and the Dark Ages. Yet we need to remember that most of these contributions would otherwise be paid in taxes (thus saving other taxpayers money); so that the Addict's charitable contribution is in some part *our* contribution, since we have to pay what he or she does not. Many of these "charitable contributions," furthermore, are not entirely disinterested. As Collier and Horowitz point out, the senior Rockefeller's charities had side effects that were quite useful to the family: creating new markets overseas, buying off public opinion, increasing oil production, disenfranchising blacks, blunting dissent, and diverting social scientists from radical analysis of the economic and political system to behaviorism and the study of social control. They estimate that 70 percent of Nelson Rockefeller's donations were "basically gifts to himself, his family, and their institutional extensions." And, finally, as we've seen, most Heavy Addicts give little or nothing to charitable causes in any case. Clearly, the reason for Addict immunity from popular resentment lies elsewhere.

As a nation we're impaled on a peculiar ambivalence. We are programmed from birth to believe that we're autonomous individuals whose actions do not affect each other. On the other hand, just like other peoples, we have an intense need for order. We want everything to run smoothly and effortlessly, with an extremely high degree of coordination which we've been trained to pretend does not exist, or at least that we're not a part of. This has led to the creation of huge mechanical structures—technological and bureaucratic—that order our environment in an impersonal, machine-like way. Our individualistic upbringings prevent us from seeing our own role in creating these structures—that they exist as a clumsy compromise between our unwillingness to live cooperatively and our need for an orderly background in which to play out our individualistic success fantasies. And since we don't see ourselves creating them, they appear as alien, oppressive forces that hem us in and block our movement. Rather than blaming the individualistic illusions that got us into this pickle, we rail at these products of our own impulses as if they belonged to someone else. The order we want is a traffic light that's always red for everyone else and green for us, and our disappointment and frustration over this leads us to glorify anyone in a position to bulldoze his way through such obstacles. A man like Howard Hughes is admired for his ability to say "Fuck you" to the government. We fail to notice that he's saying it to us as well.

Thorndike observes, in fact, that people seem "inclined to permit a rich man almost any whim except disrespect for money itself. Once in a while when a son of wealth has stood on the street and handed out hundred-dollar bills, he has been quickly committed by indignant relatives or shocked judges." Nelson Rockefeller's son Steven is commenting on the same public indulgence when he says: "There is *no* rational justification for my family having the amount of money that it has . . . the only honest thing to say in defense of it is that we like having the money and the present social system allows us to keep it."

Addicts are tolerated, in other words, not because people are stupid but because they treasure the system that fosters wealth addiction. No such system could long exist if at least a bare majority of the population were not Closet Addicts—people who entertain the fantasy that they themselves will one day strike it rich. It is this secret dream that brings the Closet Addict into unwitting collusion with the Heavy Addict, a collusion from which the Closet Addict gains nothing and the Heavy Addict everything.

The covert support of Closet Addicts maintains the oppressions of our economic system: the competitive stress, the constant striving, the unrewarding labor, the shoddy goods, the double standard of justice, the vicious circle of poverty, and so on. Closet Addicts have lost the capacity to recognize diseased behavior, preferring their secret fantasies of wealth to the real possibility of a more equitable, peaceful world. They are deaf to injustice, blind to inequality, and numb to their own exploitation, identifying with Addicts even when they take bread from their mouths ("He's just trying to make a buck like everyone else"). Closet Addicts, for example, have consistently supported lowering the capital gains tax, clinging to their distant fantasies of sudden wealth at the cost of paying real money into the pockets of Addicts in the here-and-now.

It's easy to dismiss Howard Hughes as a mere eccentric, but the difference between Hughes and the typical Closet Addict is merely one of degree. Hughes, as we have seen, was incapable of sharing or cooperating, fanatical about privacy, disturbed by any situation he couldn't control, obsessed with maintaining rigid boundaries between himself and the rest of the world, and with hiding his needs, activities, and physical processes from others. But is this unusual in a society in which so many people demand private rooms, homes, cars, laundries? Where so many people are obsessed with permanently owning every piece of equipment they might ever conceivably want to use? Where people are so nervous about boundaries and hiding their bodily processes that they invented deodorants for every conceivable part of the body, (since smells don't respect the artificial frontiers that people live by)? Where people are so blind to their interdependence that they cannot connect the polluting they do with the pollution they object to? Hughes merely carried the American Dream to its logical conclusion.

As I noted earlier, many great fortunes have been built by preying on the individualistic greed of Closet Addicts: "Look pretty," "smell pretty," "own a big car," "make a million on the stock market," "learn to dance," "eat fast," "shave fast," "learn to draw," "learn to be a computer programmer," and so on. Every city street in America screams with signs, all saying: "Make me rich! Make me rich!" Individualism makes marks of us all.

Now there are a lot more Closet Addicts around today than there were a hundred years ago—a change that has had a lot to do with our chronic inflation, as we shall see. Addicts today have a relatively benign image, although their scruples certainly haven't improved since the days of the robber barons. Indeed, the robber barons themselves are looked upon much more kindly today than they were at the time. Men like Rockefeller, Gould, and Frick were in their day almost universally detested and sometimes in physical danger from an outraged public, who knew they had caused the death and mutilation of thousands and the misery and poverty of millions.

Some of the change is due merely to the gentle veil that time throws over all past events. The victims are nameless and their tragedies so numerous that they have no meaning to us. The villains, meanwhile, have acquired a pleasing roguishness that they never had in real life. In some cases—Rockefeller, Sr., for example—this mellowing effect of time was assisted by an elaborate and protracted public relations campaign.

Nothing, in fact, seems to be easier to manipulate than public sentiment about the rich. Americans are capable of brief outbursts of rage when they hear of some extreme piece of brutality or exploitation but they are almost invariably mollified when they find that the culprit is an ordinary educated human being. We have been conditioned for a century or more of popular literary and media tradition to see villainy as a lower-class, ethnic phenomenon. Villains are supposed to look like foreigners and snarl, or laugh maniacally. When we see a plain, middle aged WASP man in a suit, with a polite soft-spoken manner and a slight paunch—obviously someone's Daddy—we feel immediately that he must have been the victim of a misunderstanding. Most Wealth Addicts are simply not recognizable as the bloated capitalists of radical cartoonists. Just as most alcoholics are not skid row bums but ordinary people who go to work every day, Addicts are ordinary people with families who happen to have a need so strong they are willing to let thousands suffer in order to satisfy it. Naturally they don't want to look at this quality in themselves and try to find ways to avoid doing so.

Nothing could better illustrate the difficulty of trying to cast Heavy Addicts in the role of Evil Money-bags than John D. Rockefeller, Jr. A timid, pious, diffident family man—the very soul of stubborn mediocrity—it was easy for him to pretend, under questioning, that he had been unaware of the terrible conditions, discussed in Chapter 4, that prevailed at his Ludlow mine, and led to the famous Ludlow massacre in which women and children were machine-gunned by hired guards. Yet he not only knew but strongly supported every move the company made, including the massacre itself. He considered the abysmal slavery of Ludlow miners as a freedom, and argued that to have a union would be to lose that freedom. He said under oath that he thought this was a great principle— worth having children shot for, worth having every miner killed. Yet it was hard for people to connect him with the slaughter of wretchedly poor women and children. "He seemed far too weak a person to have actually had a hand in making such murderous policy."

The same was true of Andrew Mellon, who bore an embarrassing resemblance to Caspar Milquetoast, the cartoon character created by H. T. Webster, and titled "The Timid Soul." It was impossible to imagine him being implicated in violence or cruelty. He was delicacy and aloofness personified. Yet he gave enthusiastic support to labor policies quite as vicious as those of Rockefeller, Jr., or Henry Ford.

This detached stance is appropriate in a way, since Heavy Addicts actually *feel* remote from the exploitation and brutality on which their wealth is based; they are, in fact, quite indifferent to it. They are just ordinary people with a desperate need, a need they feel so acutely they are incapable of responding to the misery of others. They just want the money, and this gives them an air of detachment from the brutality their desire inevitably causes.

The most important factor in increasing the number of Closet Addicts in our society was mass marketing. It was Henry Ford's invention of the notion of getting rich by selling large numbers of people things they don't need and paying them almost enough to afford them. He was perhaps the first Addict to realize that he could support his own habit by becoming a pusher.

Let me give a trivial illustration of this generalization of addiction: Most arboretums have the clearly necessary rule that flowers, shrubs, and tree branches are not to be removed, and in more placid times this rule was generally accepted. People came to them to enjoy the beauty, knowing it was always there. Recently I wandered through an arboretum on the outskirts of a large city, visited primarily by poor people. I noticed that most of them were carrying azalea branches in full bloom. When we came to the bushes themselves they looked as if they had been attacked by a deranged hedge-clipper. Clearly, to look was not enough—one had to possess, even though, as usually happens with living things, to possess was to destroy. Now middle-class onlookers to such events usually dismiss them as yet another example of the vulgarity of the poor, and flee to some more isolated locale. But the poor in this instance are merely behaving like the rich, who don't need to break branches because they can possess their own entire arboretums from which the poor are excluded. The branch-breakers are doing just what Henry Ford taught them to do by saying "Why not have one for your very own?"

We turn up our educated noses at these tenderfoot Closet Addicts and consider any place where they have appeared in large numbers as having been "spoiled." But their crime is merely to follow in the footsteps of real Addicts, who have an even stronger need to possess exclusively. After all, when a Rockefeller buys most of a Caribbean island to build an exclusive resort he is breaking off a very large branch.

Faced with our official ideology, the poor are given the option of accepting their poverty or becoming Addicts—not a very happy choice. The national ideology, in other words, says that the only way out of poverty and misery is to buy yourself out. *The poor are thereby forced to become Closet Addicts, since they are provided with no other way to define their problem.* Living under conditions that cause misery and suffering, they see money as the only escape. This is because our economic system is set up in such a way as to make no distinction between working to survive and working to support a money habit.

The best things in life *are* free, but even these can be taken from you by people with wealth and power. In nature there is food, beauty, fresh air, sensual pleasures of all kinds, satisfying work, and so on, but many of these things have been made artificially scarce by Addicts, until they have become available largely to the rich or to the deliberately poor—ex-addicts who are mostly middle-class and know how to circumvent the addictive machinery of the culture.

No one who is hungry, cold, sick, and lives in ugly and miserable surroundings is in a position to learn that money is an addiction. You might just as well lecture a desert island castaway about neurotic "joiners" who can't stand to be alone: if you ask his opinion he will tell you that being with people is a very nice thing and no one should put it down. Through this device—the forced poverty of the masses—Addicts are able to acquire popular support. *Deprivation makes fellow travelers and co-conspirators of many who are not addicts by nature.*

Once the sickness of the Addict is recognized, the dilemma of the poor can be approached single-mindedly and undistractedly. Attention can be focused not on money, but on necessity. Once necessities are available to all, everyone can be free to pursue an addiction or not, just as he or she likes. For although money can't buy happiness wealth addicts have created a society in which the lack of it can purchase pain. And this tends to confuse people into thinking that it *can* buy happiness. The obvious solution is to equalize wealth to the point where this confusion is eliminated and people can seek pleasure addictively or nonaddictively. Addicts have a right to exist—so long as their habit doesn't deprive others of the necessities of life, which at present it does.

It seems to me that any society worth talking about should be able to ensure that all its participants have adequate nourishment, warmth, shelter, some minimum level of health and safety, and the possibility of decent surroundings. A society that fails to do this isn't worth much, since some of the most primitive "savage" tribes do it with ease. Our society fails only because it has taken on, as its primary social goal, the task of fostering and supporting wealth addiction at the expense of every other human interest or goal.

There will always be differences in wealth, since some people are greedier than others. Perhaps there will always be wealth addicts. But at the moment our society is structured in such a way as to give exaggerated encouragement to these more infantile members of the population. We all suffer when we egg each other on to greater grasping, instead of enjoying the real possibility of shared resources.

Now a case can be made that criticizing the neuroses of the rich is both uncharitable and naive, since it directs energy against human beings rather than against the evil institutions that corrupt them. According to this view, we are all victims together, rich and poor alike. This is a sophisticated position, but one that lends itself better to thought than to action—appropriate perhaps for people who write learned papers about the working class in language designed to prevent working-class people from understanding them.

The problem with these "we are all victims" and "we are all guilty" arguments is that they are paralyzing. Injustices cannot be corrected without resentment. We don't have to hate Addicts but we need to resent their addiction and the misery it creates for all of us. Otherwise there is no way we can move, even in our thoughts, to correct the conditions that bring about that addiction. Permissiveness at bottom is nothing but a form of withdrawal and avoidance: "You've got your problems, I've got mine." Sooner or later the Addict is going to rip you off—his addiction demands it. To swallow your resentment at this point is to assume personal responsibility for the addict and for his addiction.

The point is not whether we are all addicts; the point is which *side* we're on. Are we for the addiction or against it? To say "we're all addicts and therefore I can't be angry at this conspicuous Addict" is not only to *acknowledge* the addict within yourself but to *support and encourage it.* To say "I may be something of an addict myself but I'm not supporting *this* turkey" is to take a stand with the healthy part of yourself and against the addictive part. To admire or indulge a Howard Hughes is not only to acknowledge the addict within you but also to give it the nod—to enter into collusion with it. Admiration of the wealth addict is a secret commitment to shoot up the first time an opportunity presents itself.

INFLATION

Inflation is the result of this diffusion of Addict attitudes throughout the population—what I call the Democratization of Greed. Capitalism works well when there is a kind of stable division of labor between cheater and cheated. It is a system founded on the following contradictory principles: (1) trade is an equal exchange based on trust; yet (2) success in trade comes from buying cheap and selling dear—i.e., from cheating, from violating that trust. Now so long as most of the population acts on Principle One, leaving only a minority of Addicts operating on Principle Two, the system can be maintained. This is likely to be the case in close, stable communities, for example, where a check is placed on most people's greed by the simple fact that they have strong and permanent ties with the people they deal with. Only a confirmed wealth addict can live comfortably with the contempt of friends and neighbors that he has cheated.

But since Henry Ford, American capitalism has begun to rely increasingly on fostering addiction in the general public—

on trying to persuade us all that we can and should seek wealth and its prerogatives. Addicts have tried to justify their addiction by making themselves heroes and models for all to emulate. Their success in this endeavor will be their downfall, however, for the democratization of greed undermines the very system that produces their wealth. As more and more people operate on Principle Two, the value of money itself begins to decline.

Inflation is now a chronic condition in our society. We no longer even talk about getting rid of it, only about reducing it. Newspapers and government officials express pleasure and relief when the *rate* of inflation declines, which is a little like saying "The weather's getting better, it's raining only a *little* more than it was yesterday, whereas yesterday it rained a *lot* more than the day before."

Since economists as a group are uninterested in people, motives, and feelings, they tend to ignore the psychological component in inflation. In the streets, heroin is progressively more adulterated—the same quantity of purchased material contains less and less of the actual drug. The same is true of money itself, the greatest drug of all. The Addict gets less and less high from the same amount of money.

Inflation is an entirely logical outcome of an economy based on greed. If too many people in a society are buying cheap and selling dear—if too many are trying to get more from barter and give less, and money is the common denominator of that barter—then all are continually getting less and less for their money. To put it another way, people put less and less effort into producing the goods and services needed for a healthy, strong society and more and more into getting the monetary rewards. But what you put in is what you get out. In the last analysis money is only a reflection of human energies: if those energies are invested solely in *generating* money, then money is all that is generated. Yet money itself is worthless, and as human energy is increasingly directed toward skimming off money and less and less toward producing anything of value, that worth-lessness becomes more and more tangible.

Suppose that I receive $50 worth of groceries from you and in exchange do a $50 repair job on your car. We pay each other. We now have the same amount of money as when we started but I have my groceries and you have your car repaired. Now let's say we both get greedy. I cut down my costs by using rusty old parts I have lying around my garage. You cut down your costs by giving me inferior produce that you were about to throw out. We each make an extra $5 profit, but I have inferior food and your car will soon break down again. With the extra money we've made we seek better service elsewhere, but since by now everyone has gotten greedy, it costs us more to get what we used to get before we got greedy. We talk about "inflation" and complain that "you can't get as much for your money as you used to."

Inflation is nothing but a thermometer of national greed. So long as there are only a few severe Addicts in the system the impact of this greed is scarcely noticeable. But when greed became a mass phenomenon it began to reflect itself in mass statistics.

If I manufacture a shoddy radio and try to sell it for the same price as I used to sell a good one, I may fail and be forced to lower the price. But if all of us are doing the same thing, prices will hold, and we'll have to pay even more to obtain the same quality we used to get. *The inflated price is a precise reflection of our greed—that is, inflation measures the exact proportion of work energy that went into greed rather than production or service. Any increase in the ratio of greed to service or production will be immediately reflected in inflation.*

This is the real meaning of inflation. Economists much prefer to talk about variations in the larger economic institutions as causes of inflation because it avoids this basic social and psychological truth. This is not to say that interest rates, taxes, government spending, the national debt structure, foreign trade, the availability of resources, and so on don't affect inflation—obviously they do. But talking about inflation on that scale protects us from looking at the fundamental flaws in the system and our own collusion in those flaws. If half my energy goes into making a product and half into trying to make money out of it, the value of that product will be more than if I put only a third of my energy into the making of it. *The more we as a people pursue money as an end in itself, the less value the money has, since we're not putting energy into the things that give money its value.*

Thus inflation has a hidden educational benefit. It teaches us what we continually try to forget: that money is purely symbolic and has no value of its own—that the pursuit of money leads to the evaporation of its value.

But there is no going back to the time when honest workers toiled incessantly for the benefit and glory of the greedy few. That innocence is lost forever. As long as our society is organized for the benefit and convenience of the greediest, the less greedy will tend to be corrupted and inflation will continue to be with us.

Inflation is the Achilles heel of capitalism. If you base an economic system on addiction, you may for a while create a flurry of energetic activity, but as more and more people join the ranks of the addicts the value of that activity increasingly declines until people are merely exchanging fistfuls of hunger and emptiness.

7

The Cure

Joy is not in things, it is in us.
CHARLES WAGNER

Capitalism and socialism are designed for children. They assume that people are incapable of mature self-government—that they must be either motivated by greed or controlled through centralized power. Many people feel enough self-hatred to agree with this assumption, but the earth abounds with negative evidence. Throughout 99 percent of our history human beings lived in small democratic bands without chiefs, without possessions, without greed; and while we have strayed a long way from that path, there are still those who follow it —not naively, as before, but with the benefit of intervening experience.

The Ego Mafia is a social fabric created solely to pretend that there *is* no fabric, while it busily creates a substitute one. As human beings seeking a livable and life-affirming environment, our best tactic is to use the Ego Mafia's own gambit against it—*to democratize the Ego Mafia and make it a more accurate map of the fabric of life: a conscious map.* At present the Ego Mafia is a stunted and malfunctioning organ, but its existence also provides us with an opportunity—the opportunity to make our conscious Egos as subtle, sophisticated, and complex as the feedback system in which our Constituents participate with other living things. This would enable us to be as in tune with natural forces as many nonliterate peoples have been, without their limitations—their vulnerability to conquest and exploitation. It would restore balance to our society and a degree of serenity to our people.

SOME OPENING MOVES

Wealth addiction is a major obstacle to this enterprise, since it locks us into the kind of frantic scrambling that makes learning next to impossible. Any solution to the problem of wealth addiction in our society must do three things:

1. Create institutions that discourage addiction.
2. Create institutions that support other motivations.
3. Increase popular consciousness about the miseries of wealth addiction and the joys that appear when it is discarded.

This book is primarily directed to the third requirement, but some attention must be paid to political structures, for without them all the consciousness raising in the world would have little impact on our lives.

One approach is to render wealth addiction as harmless as possible through a truly progressive income tax. Addicts and their congressional retainers have argued that the income tax "stifles initiative" and have succeeded in maiming it beyond recognition. Yet studies have shown that Addicts actually work *harder* with higher taxes. Thus Addicts can still devote their lives to addiction, but without thereby impoverishing the rest of the population. A truly progressive income tax would essentially be a Methadone program for the rich, protecting the innocent from the criminal fallout of wealth addiction. It is by no means a complete solution but without it no other solution is possible. The equalization of wealth is not an ethical ideal but a public health measure. By placing upper and lower limits on wealth we remove the addiction hazard from the healthier members of the population. Were we to eliminate inheritance altogether and reinstitute a truly progressive income tax, so that the money habit of the addict would not impinge upon the survival needs of the nonaddict, people would feel freer to turn their attention to more useful and rewarding pursuits.

Some will object that such proposals are a step toward traditional socialism with its huge centralized bureaucracies. This is a little like saying that if I carry an umbrella when it's raining it will cause a drought. There is nothing in tax reform requiring new bureaucracy. In fact, were we simply to eliminate all exemptions and deductions from present income tax law the size of the federal bureaucracy would be *decreased,* since collection and enforcement would both be greatly simplified.

Certainly no lasting good can come from huge government bureaucracies, just as no good comes from the huge private bureaucracies that dominate our society at present. Both of them are creations of the Ego Mafia, geared to obsessive control, a rigid binary mentality, and an unending preoccupation with security. I would be happy to see the size of both federal and private bureaucracies reduced, and have proposed methods elsewhere for bringing this about.

We are an inventive and imaginative people. We have the benefit of a long democratic tradition and an unusual tolerance for chaotic and anarchic forms of social organization. We have a rich history of decentralization, although we have spent the last several decades trying to destroy it. There is nothing to prevent our developing decentralized yet noncapitalistic solutions to our social problems. The federal government exists, ideally, only to regulate and coordinate. Most of the problems of everyday social life arise at the local level and can best be dealt with at that level.

Some people will object that greed is so basic to human beings that it's foolish to talk about structures that would significantly reduce its impact. They will point to some incident or other as proof that greed is the bottom line of human motivation. But in fact human beings are extremely varied and adaptable. There are societies in which greed is overwhelmingly important—ours is perhaps the best example—and others in which it is virtually nonexistent. Addicts usually argue that "altruistic" societies are "coercive" and "totalitarian," but this is completely misleading. In fact, authoritarian societies are usually riddled with greed because they generate such a strong feeling of scarcity. Societies in which greed is minimal are certainly cohesive and have an intense community life and commitment; given our own brand of cultural conditioning, we would probably find them difficult to live in. As a people we don't know how to express our individuality at close quarters—how to influence and let ourselves be influenced at the same time. Since we strive so hard to mask and cosmeticize our own inner natures, we feel emotionally smothered when exposed to input from others. Instead of responding, we withdraw, cutting ourselves off from the possibility of making our own voice heard. Then we compensate by trying to make a noise at a great distance—"making a name" for ourselves, or dressing in style, or buying a loud machine, or burning rubber, or any of the million other pathetic devices through which Americans assert their personal emptiness. Since we don't know how to maintain our inner equilibrium at close quarters, we would probably feel stifled in a tight, close community and run away to an alienated, greedy one. But this is only because we are brought up to believe that we are entirely separate from others—that the community doesn't include us but stands apart and over us, huge and threatening. We have a hard time recognizing that we are a living *part* of the community; that it *reflects* our influence as well as influencing us—that we help mold what it is. If such communities feel oppressive it's not because they are authoritarian (they may be intensely democratic) but because we have lost the capacity for give-and-take and can only sit on the fringe and experience what is being done to us without doing anything ourselves. To some extent this is the influence of television. Before TV, children grew up creating their own play—they knew that their enjoyment of an activity depended on the energy they invested in it. When they were in groups, they tried to move the group in directions that would express their own needs and interests, since every group is a synthesis of such inputs. Today people tend to see a group as something apart from them, which either suits them or doesn't. When it doesn't they tend to move on to some other group, like switching the channel, rather than claiming their participation and pushing for what they want. Such people feel like helpless victims in a close community, like midgets in a basketball game.

To be greedy you must feel that you are alone in some basic way. If you feel a part of a group, then what's yours is theirs and vice versa—taking from someone else is as meaningless as passing something from the right hand to the left. In close democratic societies like the Bushmen, where there are no chiefs, no hierarchies, and no concept of ownership, people share not because they are generous or altruistic, but because they feel so connected to each other that private possession is meaningless.

It's a mistake, however, to think that greed is merely something learned and can therefore be eliminated by creating the right institutions. Human beings are extraordinarily complex and adaptable. We can take countless examples from anthropology to prove that humans are either "naturally" greedy or "naturally" unselfish. In recent years people have been doing the same thing with other species, with as little point, for every conceivable social, sexual, and political arrangement that anyone has ever thought of can be proven to be "natural" by referring to some species or other, or some human society. All that anthropology and animal studies show us about human society is that *there is no baseline.* And what if there were? If chimps were less selfish than lobsters, should we strive to approximate the lobster as "more fundamental" or the chimp as "more advanced"? And if we choose the latter, why bother with animals at all? To talk of Bushmen or Eskimos or Hopi, or chimps or spiders or gorillas, or anything else outside our experience, is not to show that one thing or another is "natural," but simply to show that it's *possible*—that our own peculiar habits are not necessary and inevitable.

There are human societies (and animal ones) in which greed as we know it is virtually undetectable. All this tells us is that greed, like other human attributes, can be maximized or minimized. We have chosen, in our society, not only to maximize it but to base our entire society on it. The result has been to create a great burst of energy, unprecedented ugliness, some unique forms of human misery, and the most destructive power the world has ever known. We have touched an extreme—an extreme that centuries hence will probably be looked back upon (if there is anyone to look back), with a shudder, as a time of near-terminal illness.

Yet anything unprecedented may produce learning. We can talk about the virtues of Pygmies or Bushmen but we can't return to that innocence. All over the planet people have either succumbed to the temptations of wealth addiction or been destroyed by frustrated pushers or shoved aside into corners of the world that for the time being nobody else wanted. Wealth addiction is a powerful force. Those who have resisted it have been unable to defend themselves successfully against the irascible bullying of those who have succumbed to it. We can find only a partial answer in the Bushmen, because the Bushmen have, after all, been unable to stop us.

For the rest of the answer we have to look in the other direction—not back toward those who have never known anything but simplicity, but forward, to those who have known affluence and plenty and found it wanting. There have been such people in every advanced civilization, and their warnings and wisdom have come down to us through several millennia. Yet never before in history has any known society gone so far out on a limb or produced so many people disillusioned with wealth. If we are uniquely infected with wealth addiction we may also be the first society to develop massive antibodies to the disease. The Bushmen, after all, are simply unexposed, or luckily immune. Those who have encountered, succumbed, and transcended it are protected in a way no Bushman can ever be. The prevalence of wealth addiction in our society, and our increasing disillusionment with it, is what puts us in a position to come out the other side.

To do this we need to know not only our weaknesses and susceptibilities but also our strengths and resources. It isn't enough merely to say "I am an alcoholic"—we need also to remember all the times we got through the day without a drink. The fact is that people build homes, make clothes, raise food, create beautiful things, explore nature, build bridges, care for those who are sick, old, crazy, and helpless, make community decisions, teach, heal, and defend each other without getting paid for it, and always have. We need to create structures that will reinforce this healthy core—to create a functional equivalent of greed. It would be helpful just to make people *aware* of this health—to make them realize that people will work for things other than money. For most people, working for money is merely habitual: they do it because this is the way it has always been. They scarcely notice how much work they do that *isn't* for pay. Our society makes them feel somehow that this work "doesn't count." Only work done for money is considered "real work." But this is just Addict propaganda. With minimal reinforcement from the society as a whole, people would willingly work without pay to provide for everyone what no one should have to pay for. If the necessities of life were defined as something created by all the people and for all the people, rather than something to be bought by those who can afford it, then most of us would be safe from addiction.

There is something fundamentally wrong with a society that forces people to develop and nourish the greedy side of their characters in order even to survive. The Bushmen manage to feed themselves working less than 15 hours a week, even though *40 percent of their population* are "nonproductive," i.e., don't work at all. They live quite happily in what we would consider an uninhabitable desert, and never complain about "freeloaders."

Percival and Paul Goodman suggested years ago that everyone contribute two or three years of his or her labor to the community early in life, in return for which everyone in the society would be guaranteed a minimal subsistence. Ideally, this would be done primarily at the local level—people putting energy into projects of real importance to the neighborhood. The beauty of this plan is not merely that it frees survival from the addictive machinery, but also that it directs people's energies into the real unmet needs of the community, instead of having half of the population making gadgets nobody needs and the rest trying to persuade people to buy them.

A Gallup poll in 1978 revealed "the existence of a vast resource of volunteer citizen energy that could be used in practical ways to alleviate urban problems." The poll found that *even under our present system* two-thirds of the urban dwellers polled would be willing to devote an average of nine hours a month to serving on committees or performing neighborhood services without pay. Nine hours a month is a small amount of time, but it must be remembered that (1) these are *urban* dwellers—people who as a group are not (with the exception of a few ethnic pockets) very community-conscious; and (2) any time they donate is in *direct competition with time devoted to survival needs.* Yet even under these difficult conditions we find city people sitting on a pool of unused energy amounting to one *billion* hours a month that could be applied to pressing urban problems. Freed from the struggle to survive, the energy that would become available staggers the imagination.

THE ENEMY WITHIN

There are a hundred ways to restore some kind of balance to our society, a hundred ways to redirect our energies toward the real problems that confront us. We are not bound by any iron law of economics to devote our collective efforts as a nation to armpit odors, herbicides, bad breath, cluster bombs, and ring-around-the-collar. We can spend our time and energy in any way we want. It is true that our society is dominated by Addicts—that they control government at all levels, as well as the media, medicine, law, and academic institutions. We are surrounded by pushers. Yet they could not control us as they do were not most of us, to some degree or another, in tacit collusion with them. Ultimately it is the Closet Addict who blocks healthy change, and it is toward the cure of wealth addiction within each one of us that the rest of this chapter will be devoted.

My efforts are based on an assumption that I'd like to make clear. Wealth addiction is a planetary disease, and the planet will cure itself of that disease. All living organisms are interrelated and interdependent, and can be conceived as one democratically organized superorganism. That superorganism is extremely vital and flexible. It will heal itself. The question is, *will human beings be included in the healing?* Or will that healing take place at the expense of our species? Will we find ourselves unable to resist the impulse to blow ourselves up? Will we become an endangered species? All things live in balance or are eradicated. Will the superorganism slough us as an unfortunate and useless mutation? Or will we be tolerated as a chronic disease to be periodically doused with self-administered nuclear antibiotics?

RECONNECTING

He who knows he has enough is rich.
LAO-TZU

All addictions are more or less alike. It doesn't really matter what you're addicted to; they all involve some feeling of deficiency: "I will be complete only if I have X." I have defined addiction as a perceived hole in the self which can be filled only by taking something in from the world. Obviously, then, all cures are also alike. They all involve finding some way to say "I am complete *without* X."

Since every organism strives spontaneously toward wholeness and health, what makes addictions so stubborn? Why don't we just naturally ease out of them? The trouble with addictions is that they are self-reinforcing: if I believe that I'm not complete without alcohol, and *act* on that belief, I'm thereby telling myself—*proving* to myself—that it's true. People are constantly talking themselves into their addictions: "Six hours without a cigarette and I'm climbing the walls." We not only invent holes in ourselves, we love to put them on display.

Acting as if I have a hole in my personality is going to make me feel bad about myself, and the more I feel bad about myself the easier it is to believe in the hole. This is the familiar vicious circle of addiction: I feel bad because I drink and I drink because I feel bad. Or I shoot heroin, or accumulate money or good deeds or whatever it is I feel incomplete without. Alcohol or heroin may have particularly obvious ways of making us feel bad after a while, but any addiction eventually makes us feel empty. Even good deeds will give us a hangover if we *need* them to feel complete. As I said earlier, concentrating on any one thing tends to starve us of other things and throws us out of balance. I'm so busy trying to fill the hole in my personality that I don't take care of a variety of ordinary everyday needs that I would otherwise meet spontaneously, without even thinking about it.

Furthermore, we begin to feel worse because *the hole cannot be filled from outside.* The relief that comes from the addiction is only temporary—the relief of feeling that we're doing something about that inner void. But the feeling is illusory: the only way to fill an inner void is from within yourself. The man who makes a million dollars often feels even more empty than before: "I have a million and I'm still feeling only so-so; the hole must be bigger than I thought," and he chug-a-lugs another million. Each escalation weakens us, because it convinces us more and more of our dependence on the addiction. We find it easy to forget that we once were able to survive without any of these external props.

But how then *is* the hole filled? What is the source of the hole in the first place? To answer this we have to think back to the discussion of the Ego-despot and its relation to its Constituents. I suggested that the hole is really an illusion—an illusion that comes from the Ego's blindness: *a feeling of inner deficiency arises when the Ego is out of touch with one of its Constituents.* We are so caught up in our Ego's power game that *we imagine that the part of us that the Ego refuses to listen to isn't there at all.* The Ego is so obsessed with control that it would rather be frightened about its missing resources than feel that its rule could be dispensed with. In this the Ego is like all despotic rulers, who say, "We are weak, we need more weapons," or "we need a corridor to the sea," or "we don't have enough arable land, we must annex our neighbors." Hitler was the prototypical Ego.

One of the reasons the Ego blinds itself to its inner resources is that it wants so much to believe in its separateness. Yet its Constituents are universal. We all have within us the capacity to laugh, cry, get angry, get horny, love, hate, pursue, ignore, be weak, be strong, be brave, be afraid, be greedy, be generous, concentrate, let ourselves be distracted, and so on. To be a human being is to be all of these things. It is only the Ego that makes restrictions and sets limits to all this richness: one person "never cries," another is "always cheerful," and so on. Our Egos cripple us in this way—make us less than fully human—in response to early threats and perceived dangers: loss of the love of parents or other feared punishments. The Ego registers the danger and stops listening to all further messages from the troublesome quarter. If the Ego fears that anger would cause parental withdrawal of love, for example, or that crying would provoke parental contempt, it may stop registering those reactions altogether.

Now when this happens two things follow. First, the Ego flatters itself on its success in crippling the organism's humanness. It makes a virtue out of a limitation, priding itself on the uniqueness of the organism's handicap: "I'm even-tempered. I never get angry"; or "I'm very well organized—I pay no attention to anything in my environment that isn't on my agenda." Actually, of course, even these handicaps are not at all unique, since many people have them, but it gives the Ego a *feeling* of separateness and differentness ("I'm not like other people—have no connection with them") which helps maintain its dictatorship over the organism. (Actually we would all be unique even if we allowed ourselves to be fully human, since one person's experience can never be duplicated.)

The second result of the Ego's refusal to listen to certain Constituents is that we feel some lack, some deficiency in ourselves. The person who never cries feels hollow, cold, unable to give to people. The person who never gets angry feels weak, fatigued, and so on. The Ego's gift of feeling different from (and hence, "better than") others is bought at the price of feeling (not always consciously) *less* than others. There is no way for a human being to be more than human, but there are an infinite number of ways to make oneself *less* than human. These are illusory, of course, since the missing components are always there, but the handicaps can be very convincing both to ourselves and others.

To summarize: the Ego inflates itself by pretending that its organism is less than human, and therefore uniquely different. It ignores all reactions from those Constituents that would make the organism complete. But this makes us feel not only *cut off* from all other human beings, but *less* than they are. We become unaware of the rich resources within us. Since our Constituents are universal, we have to give up our illusion of separateness in order to fill the holes in ourselves.

Every addict feels himself or herself to be special, which is ironic because to the outsider they often look almost stereotypically alike, differentiated only by the nature of their addiction. Alcoholics tend to resemble each other, as do heroin addicts, millionaires, and so on. At another level, of course, everyone *is* special, but addicts want to be more special than anyone else, and are willing to be psychically crippled in order to hang on to that illusion. Since the specialness comes from a defect, a lack, the addict tries to have his cake and eat it too: to keep the hole that makes him special and yet at the same time try to fill it up from outside—with booze, smoke, money, power, sexual conquests, adulation, or whatever.

Once we realize that the feeling of a lack in ourselves comes, not from a real hole, but from our Ego's unwillingness to pay attention to what is there, we become suddenly aware that nothing needs to be taken in. *On the contrary, something needs to get out.* Once the blocked part of the self is expressed, the feeling of a hole or a lack or an emptiness is gone. I have experienced this personally with crying. Like most American males, particularly WASPs, I was brought up to feel that a real male didn't cry—certainly not a special being like myself. Since giving up that restriction I have often found that a feeling of emptiness that could bring me to tears would vanish with the tears themselves—that I would feel whole, energized, joyous, and ready for anything life might bring.

Obviously, crying doesn't do that for everyone and it doesn't always do it for me. It depends on which communication lines your Ego has cut—what particular form of personal pretentiousness you engage in. Women in our society, for example, are much more likely to find a feeling of fulfillment through anger—focused, direct, dry-eyed attack—since they are trained to imagine themselves to be chronically soft, yielding, and emotionally fragile. It doesn't really matter what the missing link is—when it gets reconnected and included in your circuitry the feeling of deficiency is gone.

This is the foundation of the cure of any addiction: the awareness that *there is nothing missing in your psyche. You have every trait, every emotional capacity somewhere within you. It's your birthright as a human being.* They didn't "knock it out of you." All they did was scare your Ego into severing connection with it. This hardly makes your task easy, but it at least makes it possible.

What the addict does, instead of trying to repair connections with the ignored Constituent, is to support the Ego's effort to keep it silenced by *anticipating arousal* and trying to ward it off. Alcoholics talk about "drowning sorrows," and there is this same smothering quality to all addictions. Drinking numbs many feelings. It also numbs the Ego, so that anger, tears, love, sexuality, and a host of other feelings can be released without the Ego ever having to acknowledge their presence. Wealth addiction smothers, by anticipating, insecurity—the feeling of nonsupport.

A baby cries because it is hungry, or because of some other discomfort. Normally the crying provides some relief. If it didn't cry, every discomfort would become an agonizing pain. Now suppose the ability to cry were cut off by the Ego. The child would feel a terrible emptiness and an overwhelming fear, for at any moment it could be plunged into agony from which there would be no release. A healthy solution would be to reconnect the crying response. *The addict's solution is to try to arrange the world so there is never anything to cry (or scream, or rage, or run, or fight, or love) about.* If I'm always full of food, or have daily orgasms, or am never alone, etc., etc., I'll never *need* to react in the way my Ego has made me unable to react. It never really works, of course, and requires constant, exhausting vigilance, but given the Ego's unwillingness to communicate with the exiled Constituents, it's as good a makeshift as can be found.

All addictions can be cured, then, by reestablishing contact with the exiled Constituents—letting them once again be heard from. We tend, however, to think of overcoming addictions by "conquering" them with "willpower." This is, of course, Ego-language, the language of the dictator within. Brute force and "moral fiber" are arrayed against the "enemy," which is seen as either outside oneself ("the demon rum," "the monkey on my back") or a secret insidious spy that has somehow crept inside and must be exterminated by the Ego's secret police. Far from letting the exiles return, the Ego tries to squelch the dissidents aroused by its own original repressiveness.

Many people have felt they overcame addiction by "will-power," although on balance there are probably a hundred failures for every success among those who use this approach. Furthermore, even the successes may be deluding themselves about why they *did* succeed, since the Ego has, as we shall see, a nasty habit of taking credit for all the organism's successes.

Curing addiction is not a matter of conquering but of letting go—of allowing the parts of oneself that have been silenced to emerge and fill up the emptiness. It's a completely spontaneous, though gradual process, which, given the right circumstances, will occur without any intervention from the Ego at all—no "willpower," no warring against oneself, no New Year's resolutions. Every organism wants to be whole and, *given a choice,* will move quite spontaneously in that direction.

But this qualification is the rub. No one who has ever been addicted to anything (and everyone who lives in the mainstream of America today is addicted to something) can read the preceding paragraph without protest: if it's so easy, why is it so hard?

It's hard because, without the Ego, an organism can only choose among *known* possibilities. If the Ego has limited our awareness to one kind of experience, the rest of the organism is trapped in that limitation. The Ego can envision hypothetical possibilities. The Constituents can only choose between knowns. As long as the Ego keeps the rest of the organism in the dark, no cure can take place.

The Ego *does* keep its Constituents in the dark because *it is the Ego that makes us addicted in the first place.* It's easy to forget this because the Ego is continually saying "I want you to stop this (drinking, smoking, shooting up, overeating, buying, etc.) but you're such a self-indulgent weakling that you won't." This is one of the Ego's cleverest bits of mystification, like a dictator who suppresses the press and the universities and then berates the populace for being ignorant and ill-informed: "I have to do all their thinking for them."

The organism cannot learn when the Ego never lets it have the kind of experience that will provide choice. *Once the organism has experienced what it feels like to be healthy and whole, it will move toward that state spontaneously with or without the Ego's help.* The Ego can sabotage this move toward health, as can lovers, friends, and relatives who have some vested interest in keeping the addiction going, but the impulse will always be there.

Many people have had the experience of trying to give up some addiction—say smoking cigarettes or eating candy—finding it impossible to hold out, and then giving it up a year or two later without any difficulty at all. Sometimes it just seems to drop away—no "willpower" is even required. Sometimes giving up addictions is an agony of stress and internal warfare, and sometimes it's like letting go of a rope you've been clinging to desperately for years and discovering that your feet were only a few inches from the ground. I've had both of these experiences, but also, increasingly, a third, more gradual one, in which the addiction dies a slow death with very little thought or effort or plan and many relapses. I've come to realize that giving up an addiction isn't a matter of pushing, struggling, and being heroic; it's mostly a matter of listening. At some point in the process I begin to hear that my body at times doesn't even *want,* let alone need, what I'm absorbing so greedily. Some habitual response in my head may still push me toward it, but once I can hear that tiny bit of revulsion inside, the days of that addiction are numbered. Sometimes what I can hear is simply the message "it's enough," which had before been buried under a lot of feelings of emptiness. Later, another voice is heard: I become aware of a feeling of strength and peace and sufficiency. And finally, an increasingly audible voice that's just glad to be alive. Joy can be heard only when the "holes" have been "filled"—that is, when the channels have been reopened. Joy is like a reunion among your Constituents—old friends greeting each other after a long absence, or just happy to be hanging out together.

Once I've reached this stage one of two things happens: I find I no longer even want whatever it was I was addicted to—it has lost its appeal—or I can consume it nonaddictively, that is, enjoy it when it's around, not miss it when it isn't. In neither case is any effort or compulsion involved. There is nothing I've given up that I wouldn't try again if I had the impulse.

I don't want to make curing addiction sound easy. The beginning stage is almost always difficult, sometimes excruciating, but we make it far more difficult than it needs to be. That is to say, the *Ego* makes it difficult, since the Ego is highly invested in the addiction, however much it berates us for having it.

By the same token, the Ego plays only a small part in the cure, contrary to our usual assumptions. Once the organism can *feel the alternative,* it starts its own process of moving toward it, since addiction is unpleasant and health feels good. It does this in a gradual organic way, by trial and error. We tend to dramatize this process as a great struggle between good and evil: victories for the Demon Rum or the Devil Nicotine in Acts I and III, victories for the virtuous Angel in Acts II and IV. We love to dramatize ourselves, but what is really taking place is just a health-seeking organism trying to find an optimum balance by successive approximations.

Take, for example, the idea of "relapse," which is usually viewed as a kind of tragic defeat, hopefully not permanent. Now it's quite true that many "relapses" *are* permanent and represent a victory for the despotic Ego or someone else who wants to keep the organism in a weak, addicted state. It's important to realize, however, that the "relapse" *itself* is not cause for alarm and despair, since *relapse is a natural part of the process through which an organism heals itself independently of the Ego.*

When the Constituents know in which direction health lies they begin to crawl toward it, blindly, feeling their way, through trial and error. But it's not enough to know in what direction health lies; the Constituents also need to know *how far* it is. They seek always an optimum position, which they can do only through successive approximations. This is the way a hand reaches—it may look like a straight line, but is actually a series of increasingly tiny zigzags as it zeroes in on its goal. These zigzags are not only from side to side but also forward and back—the hand overreaches, underreaches, and finally zeroes in. A *"relapse," then, is simply a "zag," an underreaching.* The Constituents try a new position, then drop back ("relapse") to check whether it's really necessary to progress that far. Since they can't "see," they have to keep feeling their way, which they can only do by comparison. Is the strange-uncomfortable-but-exciting experience of the *new* better or worse than the familiar-painful-comfortable-boring of the *old?* How *much* better or worse? Where is the optimum point? The organism has to keep comparing the experiences to find out. Furthermore, the reference points keep changing, as the new becomes less strange and uncomfortable and the unsatisfying nature of the old more clearly felt.

Supposing we are feeling our way along a continuum from 1 to 100. "One" represents total dependence on some substance, "100" is total abstinence. We start at 1, and suddenly one day experience what it's like to be at 17. We drop back to 1, but are attracted enough by the experience to try 6, which we like much better than 1. We try 12, drop back to 7 for a while. Now we're getting used to the changes, and becoming more aware of how unsatisfying 1 was. Remembering 17, we go for it, find it much more comfortable than the first time, and in a burst of enthusiasm shoot ahead to 39, then, in shock, drop back to 15, and so on. We might wind up at 100, or 50, or 20. The point is simply that without these successive trials and relapses we have nothing to compare our experience with.

People have different styles of changing. Some people take wild leaps and fall back frequently; some proceed very cautiously—2, 3, 4, 5, 6—even if their optimum might turn out to be 87. The problem with the wild leaps is that your reactions are so dramatic and noisy that you can't hear the fine tuning and don't learn anything very precise from the experience; the problem with the cautious approach is that you may never reach your optimum in your lifetime.

None of this should be taken as favoring a gradual approach to withdrawal. The underlying process of cure is *always* gradual, but your *behavior* has to be dramatic enough to provide you with a truly new experience. Most people who "cut down" on cigarettes, for example, are merely keeping the craving alive, teaching their Constituents how uncomfortable it is even to *approach* a cure, without ever revealing the pleasures of being addiction-free—tasting food, recovering your sense of smell, the feeling of lightness in the chest, and so on. It's the worst, in other words, of both worlds. Most severe body addictions have to be treated with cold-turkey cures, not because the "demon" is so strong, but because you need something this dramatic to give the Constituents enough information to change.

Change involves two parts: behaving experimentally and digesting the feedback. If you're too gradual, the Constituents don't have enough information to work with. On the other hand, if you fly frantically from one extreme to another, your Ego is providing lots of information but not giving the Constituents an opportunity to absorb it. Curing addiction requires both experimenting and listening and if either is scrimped no change will take place. Making too small a shift or too much noise are techniques the Ego uses to keep its Constituents weak and powerless.

I have found, for example, that it's usually a mistake to force myself to do any kind of physical exercise when my body is feeling sluggish and resistant. All of the minor injuries I've suffered have occurred under those conditions. (A pulled muscle, for example, is a *pushed* muscle—part of the organism straining forward, another part hanging back.) Yet at other times I find that when I actually get into the situation my body comes alive and I enjoy myself. The point is that you have to do both: to experiment against your impulse often enough to discover that it can change, and then listen carefully enough to be able to sense the difference between the sluggish feeling that evaporates under stimulation and the one that persists and leads to injuries.

I said that curing addiction was a matter of (1) experimenting with letting go and (2) listening intensely to the feedback, and I stressed the gradual, zigzag nature of change—not to encourage half-hearted experimentation but to remove the stigma from relapse and thus avoid the destructive self-trashing that so often goes with it and helps reinforce the addiction. Addictions can be cured *only* by making contact with inner sources of strength, and self-recrimination is a great impediment to this process. It's important to face the fact that you *are* addicted, but once that criticism has been made, further self-castigation and guilt are simply self-indulgent. Instead of trashing yourself for relapsing, it's better to praise yourself for lasting as long as you did. This will give you more energy for trying again, instead of wallowing in self-disgust (so long, of course, as you really listen to the new feedback). The Ego likes to look at the glass as half empty rather than half full because it doesn't want to recognize the strength of its Constituents.

This is the way your Constituents learn. This is democratic learning—what William Blake meant when he said, "If the fool would persist in his folly he would become wise." The Ego sometimes tells us to stop doing something before our Constituents have really learned how unprofitable it is. Sometimes we have to make ourselves suffer a long time before that learning takes place. And sometimes we add unnecessarily to that suffering by trashing ourselves for being stupid. In a sense Constituent learning is the only learning: despite the Ego's posing and pretentiousness it cannot by itself make us learn. It can rant and rave at us for years without having any effect except to deepen our commitment to addiction. Most of us have to listen continually to our Egos telling us to shape up in some way or another, but this just confirms our sense of having a hole in our psyche. An Ego that is willing to give "power-to-the-Constituents" doesn't criticize, it encourages. Criticalness betrays the despot, since it puts all the emphasis on what's *missing* in the organism. Every criticism by the Ego carries the secret message "without me you're nothing—weak, helpless, couldn't get along or function in the world at all." The natural response to that message is addiction: I have a hole, I must fill it. *The critical Ego, therefore, is not fighting addiction but sustaining it.* The world is full of alcoholics and other addicts who continually berate, punish, and criticize themselves and make resolutions, to no avail. When addiction is cured, it is the Constituents who bring it about. Always.

Most people don't see it this way. They see "higher motives" conquering "lower nature." They make sudden vows, and when every once in a while change does occur, they praise their Egos, ignoring the dozens of times the vows fail to have any effect. People "fight" addiction with an incredible amount of Ego-noise: the gradual scenario I described earlier is masked by the Ego's fanfare. People swear off altogether, backslide altogether, swear off altogether, backslide altogether, and perhaps eventually swear off altogether—never touching the offending substance again and insisting that if they ever took so much as a drop or a puff they'd be right back at the beginning again. Actually, in such a case, the Constituents are at a point somewhere around 55 or 60, without having any secure awareness of that fact, since the Ego is forcing them to pretend they have reached 100. Since they have no clear awareness of where they are, it's fair to say they're still addicted. "Once an addict, always an addict" is the Ego's way of keeping despotic control, keeping the organism feeling it has a hole in its psyche. Usually these kinds of "ex-addicts" get addicted to something else—something less visible, more socially acceptable.

Even when the cure is real and complete the Ego tends to take credit for it. It says, "You still aren't complete, because

I made you well. *I* overcame your weakness. You still *want* to be an addict but I've saved you." In this way much of the benefit of the cure is lost. The truth is that *you couldn't possibly have given up an addiction unless you yourself—your Constituents— spontaneously wanted to.* Don't give credit where credit isn't due. Remember that your Ego has been criticizing you for years (and criticizes some people all their lives) without having the slightest impact. The credit belongs solely to you and is testimony to your increasing wholeness.

Now, up to this point I have assigned the Ego the role of the heavy in our drama of human redemption, and it is usually quite true that the Ego's contribution is for the most part negative. Yet this need not be the case, as I suggested in Chapter 5: the Ego can be democratized and taught to play a helpful role. Furthermore, in one important respect the Ego has a function that is not only positive but essential. Most addiction cures would not even begin without the Ego's intervention.

The reason for this is very simple: our Constituents learn by feeling their way, through trial and error, toward an optimum position between *known* alternatives. The Constituents cannot envision a hypothetical possibility. Only the Ego can do this. The Ego can see alternatives, and because of that can experimentally place the organism in a new situation ("cold turkey," for example), thus providing a new option for the Constituents to use in their groping toward health. Until the organism has actually *experienced* the alternative no movement or choice by the Constituents is possible.

The reason addictions are so difficult to cure, then, is because the Ego, which we almost invariably rely on to get us out of trouble, is both essential for getting things moving and a major obstacle once we're under way. Like every leader who ever lived, it acts sometimes for the good of the whole and sometimes selfishly, to preserve its own power position. When the people are strong and vigilant they can tell the difference—support the leader when he or she is helpful, oppose and correct the leader when he or she is arrogant. A good leader is the servant of the people, and a good Ego is the servant of its Constituents.

It doesn't take great cleverness to tell whether your Ego is being helpful or self-serving. The Ego that berates and criticizes you all the time wants primarily to maintain its own despotism. The Ego that encourages you to try new behavior and take reasonable risks is a good servant-of-the-people. For most of us, of course, it isn't as clear-cut as that; our Egos are ambivalent—combining criticism and encouragement, severity and flexibility. A good criterion to use in assessing your Ego's performance is rigidity. A despotic Ego takes a harsh moral stance. It spouts ideology and talks of purity and abstinence and absolutes. It pushes you when you feel weakest. A democratic Ego is experimental, curious, venturesome, and thoughtful. It catches you when you're strong and says, "Try it now!"

It isn't the content of what the Ego says but the style: a despotic Ego is always operating on some kind of rigid principle. *It doesn't matter whether the principle is ascetic or hedonistic, the despotic Ego is guided by a rule rather than a flexible response to the situation, to others, to Constituents.* An Ego-driven organism is bureaucratic—it has rules that it applies to every occasion. It loves "always" and "never." It either "doesn't touch" or "can't refuse," regardless of whether it wants or doesn't want at any given moment. Sometimes this can be a little tricky: many despotic Egos have learned a little Gestalt psychology or partaken of some of the bourgeois spiritualism so popular today. They have developed a rigid rule of "doing what I feel like" or "going with the flow" which somehow manages to be completely mechanical and devoid of spontaneity despite the surface intent. Hedonism is just a "bread and circuses" approach to the Constituents—the Ego makes controlled gifts to them without in any way sharing power. The despot's hand is revealed by the individualistic style: the commitment is to *"my"* pleasure. But Constituents are part of a universal community—

they don't see the world in terms of "mine" and "thine." Any "mineness" in behavior shows that the Ego is still dictator. The same holds for bourgeois spiritualism: if a person is preoccupied with his or her own *individual* enlightenment or spiritual development, the Ego is still enthroned, still determined to achieve "specialness" by being less than human. Its rigidity, consistency, and indifference to others reveal that some of its Constituents are being denied awareness.

WEALTH AND SIMPLICITY

Any attempt at poverty which is not voluntary defeats the end which is freedom—freedom from the slavery of matter.
SWAMI VIVEKANANDA

I have tried to show, in a variety of ways, that a democratic, flexible organism doesn't waste time trying to set itself apart from other organisms—that the Constituents of one organism are aware that they are indissolubly linked with the Constituents of all other organisms. It is only the most despotic Egos that are obsessed with standing apart in isolated pomposity. This, of course, is only a pose, for in fact all Ego-despots are pretty much alike in their fears, their arrogance, their parasitic dependence on their Constituents, and their denial of that dependence. But our Addict economy depends upon our seeing ourselves as heroic isolates and tells us every day that we are separate and alone ("divide and conquer")—competing in a million ways with each other, inadequate in all of them, desperate for love and approval. It insists—through mass media, medicine, psychiatry, and law—that our difficulties in life are merely personal.

Yet to take the traditional Marxist position and say they are not *also* personal is to make exactly the same error. For since the Constituents are universal and interconnected, the personal and the political are one and the same. Your internal problems, my internal problems, and our social problems are all one problem.

The first duty of a leader is to the people, and the first duty of an Ego is to its Constituents. But since there is no difference between "its" Constituents and all other Constituents, the Ego's service is properly directed to *all* Constituents everywhere. Only a democratic Ego, however, is equally generous and protective to its own Constituents and those of others. Some Egos assume the posture of "unselfishness," ignoring their own Constituents to serve other people. Others make self-indulgence a matter of ideology, flattering their own Constituents and spitting on everyone else's—as if obnoxiousness were in itself proof of enlightenment. The second group is arrogant in assuming that enlightenment is a private affair, the first in assuming that interdependence must be created by an act of will. Both approaches are hoaxes, for in both cases the Ego merely serves and inflates itself. A true democratic spontaneity and generosity of spirit would not exclude either one's own Constituents or those of others—would not, in fact, make any great distinction. *The fact that so sharp a demarcation is made between one's own Constituents and all others betrays the influence of a despotic Ego,* for only the Ego is preoccupied with such distinctions. *If the Ego does not attend to other Constituents, it isn't genuinely attending to its own, and vice versa.*

Our society trains us to be addicts—to deal with stresses and strains by buying or ingesting something, rather than by expressing or balancing ourselves. The hero of a Hollywood film, or TV series, confronted with an upsetting situation, says, "I need a drink," rather than expressing what he feels about it. A drag on a cigarette helps him stall for time so he can falsify his response to a question. Children are taught very young— and not merely by advertising—that the appropriate response to "the first sign of stress" is to take something in—to drink or take pills when upset, buy cosmetics when shy, get a car when feeling inferior, and so on. Yet every time we follow this advice the conviction that we have holes in ourselves deepens.

Every year psychiatrists write articles about why people become depressed and suicidal around Christmas time. They talk about memories of childhood and disappointed expectations, and other things that leave unscathed the basic tenets of our addictive culture. But it should be obvious by now that people get miserable at Christmas because it's a time when they are forced to concern themselves with (1) what they don't have and (2) what they will give to others. "What do you want (lack) for Christmas?" People make jokes around this: "my two front teeth," "a happy family, no quarreling for once," "my youth," and so on. The word "want" means both desire and poverty: people at Christmastime could reasonably be said to be "in want." Christmas is the biggest holiday most Americans celebrate, a very appropriate holiday (in the form it now takes, at least) for a society based on wealth addiction.

Many people have trouble seeing wealth addiction the same way they see alcoholism or drug addiction. For them addiction is weakness and indulgence and while buying and spending can be fitted into that framework, other aspects of wealth addiction—the planning, the cautious accumulation, the drive to achieve, the discipline—seem very different from alcoholism or heroin addiction. Many a poor alcoholic's wife has wished for nothing so fervently as that he would turn overnight into a wealth addict.

Every addiction has its own side effects, but whether they give off the appearance of weakness or strength, discipline or indulgence, is quite irrelevant to the intensity of the addiction itself. Whether a person is unable to work hard at anything or unable to *stop* working, he or she is still addicted. As I pointed out in Chapter 3, the Ego may insist that safety lies in always being sloppy or in always being tidy. It's the "always" that betrays the dictator, and it's the "always" that reveals an addiction. Whether it is alcohol, or praise, or money, or status, if a person must have it to feel whole, then he or she is addicted.

To the person who enjoys life the apparent self-discipline of the "workaholic" seems very impressive. Speaking as an exworkaholic, I can assure the nonaddict reader that no great "strength of character" is involved. Work can be an escape and an indulgence like anything else, and I found that I used it that way for many years. Picking up an uncompleted task involved no more strength of character than turning on the television. Through constant work I was able to evade difficult decisions, complex interpersonal encounters, and myself. It was like reading an endless and enjoyable novel without having to feel guilty. Giving it up required much more strength since I had to face up to who I was and what I wanted, how I was connected with others and what I was doing with my time. As I began to deal with these issues I realized that 90 percent of my constant work had been waste motion, useful only to keep me in the essentially drugged condition of being "hard at work."

Work can still be very enjoyable to me. I like challenge and like to feel useful. But to be enjoyable it has to take its proper place among many other activities and interests. A large project, like a book with a deadline, can trip me into my old habits on occasion, but I no longer find it pleasurable. I have the most profound conviction, as I'm slaving frantically away, that to a large extent I'm wasting time. And when I look back over what I've produced on those occasions of heroic effort, even my critical Ego is forced to agree with that intuitive judgment, and I spend hours undoing what I spent weeks doing.

People like to do what they do with some degree of skill. They want to get good at it. This may involve a certain degree of passion and commitment hard to discriminate from addictive ambition. We can distinguish between them by looking at the goal: is the energy invested in the activity because it's an end in itself or a means to an end? Do I do it because I love doing it well and have an image in my mind of what it would feel like to do it even better? Or do I do it because I have an image of the money I'll make or the recognition and applause I'll receive? If my fantasies revolve around being a star or getting rich, then the activity is merely in the service of addiction.

Most people, of course, have to struggle just to survive. They work because they have to, and their labors are relieved neither by satisfaction with what they do nor with images of future success. They don't enjoy the luxury of choosing between work that is inherently satisfying and work that is just a means to an end. But even middle-class people who have such choices often feel as if they were compelled from outside, and it is these driven, compulsive wealth addicts who create a world in which nonaddicts must slave to survive. Misery loves company.

Like all addictions, wealth addiction is self-reinforcing. It creates habits of mind and habits of behavior that keep us from seeing the way out. By emphasizing our dependence on externals, for example, it weakens our self-respect. We lose the feeling that we could survive or care for ourselves without the trappings of civilization—we feel incompetent, helpless, and then have to use money and status to prop ourselves up. Furthermore, by locking us into ownership, distracting us and keeping us busy with janitorial services for our possessions, wealth addiction makes it harder and harder for us to see our lives in perspective—see that we actually *have* choices. Possessions multiply: each one requires accessories for maintenance, enhancement, protection, and so on, so that each purchase traps us into further ones. We begin to see our lives as a matter of necessity and compulsion rather than choice—we feel we have to work and scramble just to "keep up" (sometimes literally in the form of credit payments). And finally, wealth addiction, with its competitiveness, its concern with surfaces—with appearance, status, prestige—produces a less open, more masked life-style, which in turn fosters loneliness and suspicion. The fact that we have to hide parts of ourselves makes us feel empty and unloved and we seek more wealth to fill this hole.

But I don't want to create an impression of an overwhelming monolithic force (an old Ego Mafia trick to discourage change). Like every system, our wealth-addictive society is both self-reinforcing and self-undermining. We can see this by looking at advertising: everyone knows that commercials foster addiction; what is less obvious is that they also tend to cut the ground from under the system that created them.

A commercial captures our interest by associating its product with something desirable—beauty, success, health, sex. But with so many competing bids for our attention, successful ads have to touch deeper and deeper needs and desires in order to stand out. Ultimately they have to tap into those hungers that are created by the addictive economy itself, and at that point the whole process begins to backfire.

Every ad that tries to associate a product or company with something the viewer feels is desirable carries a double message: (1) that the product can be associated with X (something desirable) and (2) that X is, in fact, desirable. This may seem harmless enough—presumably the viewer already knows X is desirable or the advertiser wouldn't be using it to sell his product. Yet it often has subtle consequences. Suppose, for example, a corporation tries to associate itself with ecological consciousness, as many of the major corporations (usually the worst polluters) are now doing. Initially the message is a bold-faced lie. Yet it represents a sharp departure from the position corporations used to take, that they were in business solely to make a profit. The second message in such an ad is that "it is a desirable thing for a corporation to be ecologically conscious." Corporations now begin to compete in presenting themselves in this way. As the competition escalates, corporations begin setting up little demonstration projects they can show off to the public and photograph for their ads. Executives in charge of such projects are put in the position of having to make their reputations as managers by being more ecologically sophisticated and creative than anyone else, and so on. There is always a certain pressure on an oft-told lie to make it come true retroactively, and in the meantime the public is being educated to expect ecological responsibility from corporations, which is presumably the last thing the corporations want.

Another example has to do with being in nature and enjoying informal group activities. TV ads have constantly tried to associate cigarettes, beer, soft drinks, automobiles, and other products with these "natural" pursuits. But again, the second message—"it's good to be in the country, or to play informal games in groups, or just to hang out with people"—can backfire. The result of these constant reminders has been not only to sell a lot of beer and cola but also to remind people that there are a lot nicer things to do than sit in front of a TV set. (Viewers may have gotten the message, for TV viewing has dropped measurably for the first time in its history.) In its desperate search for unsatisfied longings, the advertising industry may have stumbled onto the very things that will begin to free viewers from addiction.

This doesn't mean we can all lie down and let nature take its course. We all recognize the need for some kind of personal human commitment in dealing with wealth addiction—what William James called a "moral equivalent of war." It's fascinating to me how often this phrase is quoted by news commentators and academics as if James had merely expressed a yearning for such an equivalent—as if the search were still on. But in fact James *found* the "moral equivalent of war" and had quite a bit to say about it: "May not voluntarily accepted poverty be 'the strenuous life,' without the need of crushing weaker peoples? Poverty, indeed, *is* the strenuous life—without brass bands or uniforms or hysteric popular applause or lies or circumlocutions; and when one sees the way in which wealth-getting enters as an ideal into the very bone and marrow of our generation, one wonders whether a revival of the belief that poverty is a worthy religious vocation may not be 'the transformation of military courage,' and the spiritual reform which our time stands most in need of."

All personal solutions to wealth addiction involve one form or another of what has come to be called Voluntary Simplicity.

This does not necessarily mean going "back to nature," and it does not mean living in poverty and discomfort, although some people may elect forms of simplicity that would be highly uncomfortable to the rest of us. Above all, it doesn't mean forcing yourself to give up something you really enjoy, out of some pious conviction that it's the "right thing to do." Voluntary Simplicity merely means trying to rid one's life as much as possible of material clutter so as to concentrate on more important things: creativity, human survival and development, community well-being, play. It involves unhooking ourselves from the Ego Mafia—from the huge bureaucracies that control so much of our lives—and celebrating our connection with other living things, especially each other. It involves rearranging our lives to a more human scale and adjusting our ecological fine tuning.

The key word in Voluntary Simplicity is "voluntary," which means that the giving up of material clutter is not coerced either from the outside or from the inside. As André Vanden Broeck observes, only those who have experienced affluence are in a position to have a "choice divorced from need." The poor aren't in a position to make such a choice—they are stuck with a scarcity that is neither simple nor voluntary.

Nor is Voluntary Simplicity coerced from within, for to deprive yourself out of some ideological conviction is merely to feed the Ego Mafia. The word "simplicity" may have overtones that arouse our suspicions: a vaguely puritan ring, conjuring up images of drab smocks, self-righteousness, and flagellation. But if this is the spirit in which Voluntary Simplicity is embraced the result will most certainly be noxious. There is an old Zen story about two monks traveling together who encounter a nude woman trying to cross a stream. One of them carries her across, much to the consternation of the other. They continue in silence for a couple of hours until the second monk can stand it no longer. "How," he asks, "could you expose yourself to such temptation?" The first monk replies, "I put her down two hours ago. You're still carrying her."

Addiction is internal: if you experiment sincerely with Voluntary Simplicity and find yourself still thinking of money and possessions, your simplicity is a fraud and you might just as well go back to pursuing wealth until you've had your fill of it.

To achieve its goal, Voluntary Simplicity must be undertaken in the spirit, not of puritanism or self-flagellation, but of adventure. All adventurers throughout history have, after all, been people who abandoned comforts, possessions, love, and security to seek new experiences in faraway places. We don't think of them as puritans but as bold seekers and risk takers, and the same spirit often infuses those who embrace Simplicity today. Simplicity need not be Spartan or self-denying. People are always asking "Why can't life be simple?" or "Why is my life so cluttered?" or "Why can't I find a little peace?" This yearning is what Voluntary Simplicity is all about. Richard Gregg, who coined the term in 1936, once complained to Gandhi that while he had no trouble giving up most things he couldn't let go of his books. Gandhi told him he shouldn't try: "As long as you derive inner help and comfort from anything, you should keep it." He pointed out that if you give things up out of a sense of duty or self-sacrifice they continue to preoccupy you and clutter your mind.

To talk of "denying oneself" is to use the language of despotism. Simplicity is an affirmation, not a denial of oneself. We need to remember that wealth addiction exists only because the Ego has denied parts of the self and tried to fill the gap with money. To let go of any piece of your money habit is to affirm and liberate those parts of yourself.

People have always resisted this idea, partly through humor ("The best things in life are free but I'll settle for second best"; "Money isn't everything but lack of money isn't anything"), and the immediate response of 9 out of 10 people when they first hear the title of this book is some version of: "I only wish they'd give me enough to *get* me hooked." Humor is a good antidote to the priggishness of those who embrace poverty out of some ideological fervor, but it clouds the fact that Voluntary Simplicity is just a way of having a happier, freer life.

But if Voluntary Simplicity is so enjoyable and natural, and wealth addiction so frantic and crippling, why don't people give it up spontaneously? Why do people cling to it? Why do we need to talk about it at all if there's no need to push ourselves?

There are two answers to this. The first is that people *are* giving it up spontaneously. A report from the Stanford Research Institute estimated that 5 million Americans are engaged in Voluntary Simplicity and predicted that the number would reach 35 million by 1985. They also estimated that from one-third to one-half of the population was "sympathetic" to the movement. This report aroused more interest among corporate leaders than any previous report of Stanford's Business Intelligence Program, perhaps not too surprisingly, since it predicted that "the fastest growing sector of the market is people who don't want very much."

The second answer is that people don't really know how it will feel to give something up until they try, and (like the man clinging desperately to the rope with his feet only a few inches from the ground) things look very different on one side of that experiment than they do on the other. I said earlier that the Ego plays an important role in being able to consider hypothetical alternatives and set the natural process in motion—if this weren't true, there would be no point in writing this book. Sometimes giving up wealth addiction and moving toward Voluntary Simplicity occurs quite spontaneously, like a snake sloughing its skin, or like discarding a winter garment when spring comes. But more often there's a lot of thought involved, a lot of weighing of alternatives, a lot of internal dialogue about it. In short, more often than not, the Ego gives the push that sets the whole thing in motion.

The proper role of the Ego, as we have seen, is to get you to *experiment,* to *try* it. If it's insisting that you make some *permanent* sacrifice, either for the good of your private soul or for the benefit of humanity, then it's probably trying subtly to scare you off and maintain the addictive status quo.

The key is experimentation. It doesn't really matter *why* people try it. Some people like to take risks; some want to feel more independent; some like to feel virtuous; some do it for fun; some are pushed into it by their Egos. Many try it out of some ideological conviction and only later discover that it's enjoyable.

Once you try giving up something, the important thing is to listen to how it feels, so your Ego can process the information and work with you rather than against you. At first it's hard to hear over the noise of your anxiety, your Ego's loud alarm-system. The more you experiment the more your Ego relaxes and the more you can hear of your inner self. And the more of your inner self you can hear, the more your Ego relaxes.

Voluntary Simplicity, like letting go of any other addiction, seems frightening and repellent at first because you imagine yourself taking your hunger with you into an empty situation. Since you already feel tense trying to fill that emptiness, it seems positively repulsive to think of trying to get along without those props. But one of the very first things that happens as you experiment is that you discover unsuspected strengths (if you don't, then you're not ready to start). You begin to feel that you have a choice to be addicted or not, and that in itself is strengthening.

The next thing that happens is that you find yourself at times not even wanting whatever it is you're addicted to. This doesn't mean your desire for it has necessarily decreased—merely that your Ego is much more tuned in to its Constituents, much more aware of fluctuations in mood and taste. The most confirmed alcoholic has moments when he doesn't really *feel* like drinking, but drinks anyway because his anxiety, his desire to be drunk, and his belief in his addiction drown out that inner sensation. Sometimes the drinking itself serves to drown out that latent disinterest in drinking. This is why alcohol is such a popular addiction—it numbs you to your moments of health.

A cigarette commercial some years ago asked, "Are you smoking more lately and enjoying it less?" Designed merely to persuade smokers to switch their brand, this ad was the subject of endless parody. It obviously touched a chord of some kind in the American psyche—one which at the time could be dealt with only through humor. This chord is simply that addiction is not really satisfying. Pleasure and compulsion may not be mutually exclusive but they're quite incapable of a lengthy marriage. The obvious (though utterly un-American) solution to "smoking more and enjoying it less" is to smoke less . . . and enjoy it more.

What happens when you begin to let go of an addiction is that you find that some of the time you don't want whatever it is that hooks you, and that if you avoid it at those times you enjoy it more when you *do* indulge. This is all a part of tuning into those heretofore stifled Constituents, absorbing their input, welcoming them as full participants in that chaotic community we call a human being.

This is why the weaning from addiction, if it's done in a nonpuritanical way, tends to create pleasure and a feeling of fullness. It's a bit like what happens when people start exercising with an eye to holding down their weight. At first they may actually eat more, but after a time they usually find that the more they exercise the less they feel a compulsion to eat. This is because the exercise activates and energizes the whole body, and makes the person aware that the body is whole and complete and functions well—rather than being an empty sack with a hole in it, constantly draining.

Wise men and women in every major culture throughout history have maintained that the secret of happiness was not in getting more but in wanting less. But somehow this has never been presented in a very appealing way. It is usually said in the context of such extreme spiritual detachment that one feels, "Well, that may be appealing to *him,* but I'm just an earthier person than that." But in fact this principle has nothing to do with being spiritual; it has to do with being happy. When people feel really joyful—just glad to be alive—it isn't because they've won a washing machine on a quiz show, or been promoted, or underbid a competitor on a contract. It's because they feel good about being who they are—as is, complete, *not wanting anything.* Joy, in other words, comes from *nothingness.*

The reason for experimenting with Voluntary Simplicity is that it brings excitement, challenge, and joy: as your possessions get smaller, you get bigger. It's probably wise to give up only as much as feels good, and then try more when you're ready, but, as in everything else, if there is no risk at all, there probably won't be much payoff. At some point you have to take a leap and find out what it's like to do things very differently from what you would have planned.

My own limited foray into Voluntary Simplicity has been one of the happiest experiences of my life. For while I am certainly a long way from Diogenes, I live now on less than one-fourth of what I lived on a few years ago, and this doesn't take inflation into account. Yet I feel that my life is not only simpler and freer but also more luxurious, in the sense that I spend money freely on the things I enjoy and feel as if I have not only enough of what I want, but a great abundance. When I worked hard and had a large income I felt deprived of many things. Now that I have very little I live like a king (at least in my own eyes) and it's a rare day that I'm not consciously grateful for my good fortune.

I can't claim that all of this was by my own doing. On one occasion my progress was given a considerable nudge by an unexpected and severe financial setback. But even at that point the option to triple or quadruple my income was open to me, and although I had a very difficult time of it for several months, the satisfactions of my life were so great that I never gave it serious thought.

I also don't want to give the impression that I'm living in a hut in the mountains, chopping my own wood and living on berries. I live in a small but pleasant apartment in a small city. I own two or three things worth stealing. I eat in good (though mostly inexpensive) restaurants whenever I feel like it, which is usually two or three times a week. For the last several years I have lived on an income that most middle-class Americans would classify as "poor," yet I can recall very few times during that period when I denied myself any kind of food, drink, clothing, or shelter, however luxurious, because of lack of funds. This has been possible for several reasons. I don't own a car or any major appliances. Some of the time I have shared living space with others. It's also true that expensive clothes and hotels don't interest me very much, and that I'm not attracted to environments where people go to parade their wealth or status. But I'm not at all ascetic by nature, and I find I'm freer to spend money without thinking than I was when I made three times as much.

I am not offering my own experience as a model to readers: my tastes and my circumstances are different from yours. Things that are easy for me to do without are hard for others, and things that I cling to, others are able to relinquish without stress. The goal is to find your own ways of simplifying and freeing your life, for only *you* know what's easy and what's hard. No one can tell anyone else *where* or *when* to cut down. The experiment is voluntary and the techniques must be developed by trial and error.

Take, for example, the automobile. I have not owned a car for eight years, although I've lived for about half of that time with people who did, and therefore had some access to one. Not owning a car has given me more freedom than any other single form of "renunciation." It has also saved me more money. I have a good memory for what car ownership used to cost me, and therefore always feel comfortable renting a car or taking a taxi when it seems convenient. Most of the time, however, I ride a bike or walk—not to save money but because I enjoy it. Once I got accustomed to biking, riding in a car on a nice day felt to me just like being inside: cooped up, confined.

Ivan Illich calculates that the average American devotes more than 1,600 hours a year to his or her car—sitting in it, taking care of it, earning the money to pay for it—*forty full work weeks* a year. Yet in that time he or she travels only about 7,500 miles, so that the net result of all that effort is the ability to go five miles for every hour of effort, which is about what can be done walking or biking. This, of course, takes no account of the environmental cost or the damage an automobile does to our health and the good done by walking or biking. It would be hard to find a mass consumer item in our society more expensive, wasteful, destructive, and ultimately futile than the automobile.

Yet many people would rather drive to a hut than walk to a mansion, and our entire society is structured to fit that preference. In many places living without a car is a great hardship. I'm not interested in people adopting any *particular* form of Voluntary Simplicity: some people have two pickups and no electricity or indoor plumbing. My goal is only to persuade people to experiment with what feels possible for them.

I would, however, like to suggest four broad guidelines that might help in those explorations.

1. *Listen to what's going on inside.*   How do you feel after you've bought something? Is it really satisfying? Does it make you feel good? How does your work make you feel? Would you do it if you weren't getting paid and had enough to live on? Pay attention to the times when you feel happy. Was money involved? If so, in what way? Tuning into our feelings around money is harder than it sounds, since our culture tells us so constantly (through game shows and lottery winner interviews, for example) how we're *supposed* to feel.

Listening to the inside is a skill that can also be sharpened by listening more carefully to the outside, since they are, after all, part of the same fabric. Close your eyes every now and then and listen to the sounds around you, and find out just how strong a role the Ego Mafia plays in your own life. How much of what you hear is wind and birdsong and how much is the buzz of motors and the clash of metal? How much celebrates life and nature, and how much merely advertises someone's power or glorifies somebody's Ego? A more acute awareness of the external sounds that impinge upon you will heighten your awareness of your own Constituents and, of course, vice versa.

2. *Try to minimize your dependence on large, impersonal bureaucratic systems over which you have no control.* One of the definitions of Voluntary Simplicity is trying to live your life on a human scale, making your community small enough to comprehend and deal with effectively. This might mean, for example, not owning anything that you couldn't repair yourself, or that couldn't be repaired by a friend or neighbor that you trust. It might mean buying goods and services only from small firms known to you. It might mean avoiding any form of institutional indebtedness or credit, which ties you into an enormous bureaucratic system. It might even mean disconnecting yourself altogether from large utilities—from electricity, oil, gas, telephones, and so on. This would, of course, be difficult for all but the most ardent "back-to-nature" enthusiasts, but it isn't as outlandish as it sounds. Migration back to the land is a major population trend in every part of the country, and a significant fraction of these people are happily "roughing it."

Early in 1978 a small town of 2,500 people in northern California went on a voluntary week-long total power blackout to protest their high utility bills—switching to oil lamps, candles, camping stoves, and ice chests. Almost everyone experienced these very real discomforts as a positive event. The blackout "brought everybody in town closer together. . . . Instead of watching the boob tube all night, we're getting out and visiting each other. And people are helping people." There were frequent potlucks, and people shared makeshift facilities. "We're all talking to each other more and I have never seen things so good in Westwood." An adolescent girl observed that at first "a lot of kids like me missed things like the hair dryers," but "now that nobody is using them—or television sets—we don't miss them anymore."

The great blizzards that hit New England the same winter seemed to have had the same effect. Streets in paralyzed cities were filled with people as if on a holiday, brimming with high spirits and friendliness. This was particularly noticeable in Cambridge, Massachusetts, where people are so in love with their automobiles that they'll drive a few blocks through continuous traffic jams and then circle irritably for fifteen minutes looking for a parking space, rather than subject themselves to a peaceful five-minute walk (then, to take off the fat this puts on, they jog through the city, gulping lead, carbon monoxide, and sulfur dioxide into their lungs). People were so happy in the empty streets that when the first cars began to appear they were booed and even occasionally stoned. Newspapers for months afterwards carried editorials, columns, letters, and articles commenting on how blissful the city was without cars, and couldn't we somehow manage to create the same effect without a blizzard? But old habits are hard to break, especially when an entire sick, failing, and desperate economy seems to depend on persuading people to keep a monetary needle dangling from their arms at all times.

I should perhaps reemphasize that these guidelines are intended to help free you from addiction to money. They are in no way to be taken as good financial advice, although they may turn out to be good *survival* advice. For example, I suggested unhooking yourself from credit systems, but this should be done in full knowledge that anyone who doesn't borrow in a time of inflation is losing money. On the other hand, as I observed earlier, it seems pointless to worry about losing something that's rapidly becoming worthless anyway.

3. *Avoid Moneythink: buy things only because you want or need them, never because they are cheap.* When you let your thoughts drift into concern about what the "best deal" is, you're sliding into Moneythink. You are letting your spirit be dominated by a system that has nothing to do with you as a person—that doesn't care what you want, and is not designed to benefit you or to make you happy. If I want a red coat, what does it matter to me that the "best buy" is a green one? Information is useful, of course, but if you can't understand what you're buying without reading a lot of manuals and research reports, you're probably unwise to want to own it in the first place.

Moneythink tells you that who you think you are and what you want is of no importance—that you are simply part of a huge machine and motivated solely, like all the other parts, by a desire to maximize your money. A recent *New Yorker* cartoon, for example, showed a middle-aged couple on a beach bundled up in fur coats; the man is saying "Don't think of the discomfort—think of the low rates."

When money is used merely as a tool it comes in only at the *end* of a train of thought: you think how you want to spend your day—what you want to do—*then* you think whether any money is required to do it. The wealth addict thinks about the money first: what to buy or own, how to use the money he already has, how to get more. What the wealth addict wants to do is controlled by the money itself or the lack of it. The money is in his thoughts from the very start.

This question of sequence is vital. A man who takes a painkiller because of an acute injury is not at that point an addict. An addict is a person who takes a painkiller to start the day. Money is supposedly a tool: you don't walk through life with a wrench in your hand looking for nuts and bolts to twist—you leave it in a toolbox until you need it, and otherwise never think about it. A healthy person would treat money the same way.

4. *Never own what you rarely use.* We like to fill our dwellings with objects that "might come in handy," equipment for events that occur a few times a year, clothes for "special occasions." New products are invented literally every day, most of

them absurdly specific. But what harm is there in being thus prepared for every conceivable eventuality? It may make for a lot of clutter (so much so that people often either forget where they've put things or forget they even have them and buy more) but what difference does that make if people like living that way?

The problem is that the choice is not always a free one. There are few people who can surround themselves with material possessions and not be bound by them. Having chosen repeatedly to prepare yourself against all future contingencies, it isn't too likely that you'll be able to walk away from your possessions or treat them lightly. Your life becomes tied to matter—a wall of possessions barricades you against the kinds of experiences that challenge you, change you, and lift your spirits. You have all these possessions to avoid being caught short, to avoid hassle and discomfort. Yet the process of avoiding some hypothetical *future* discomfort ties you to a chronic nagging level of real *present* discomfort.

What would happen if you were caught not owning something when you wanted to use it? You could buy it then, or borrow it, or rent it (for you can rent virtually anything today), or do without it. In any case the trouble would be confined to the day it arose instead of pervading every day of your life. It might even provide you with an interesting experience.

Most of the "joys of ownership" turn out to be a tiresome bother. Hugh Hefner, for example, whose passion for possession has managed to make even sex boring, owns his own private DC-9. One of his associates points out that because of this "convenience" Hefner can't just hop on a plane and go where he feels like going. He has to plan every trip several days in advance—arrange for pilots, food, flight schedules, and so on. To be an owner, as I said before, is to be a servant, and if you're eager to serve, why not serve living things?

There is evidence that Americans are on the brink of radical changes in life-style. A Harris poll in 1975 showed that 90 percent of the population would happily eliminate annual changes in clothing fashions and car design and other "givens" of our way of life. In fact, given a choice between continuing inflation and a basic alteration of our "waste and growth" life-style, Americans opt for life-style change by a ten-to-one margin. Another Harris poll, in 1977, showed most Americans thoroughly disillusioned with growth and materialism. Almost 80 percent wanted less emphasis in our society on reaching a higher standard of living and more emphasis on learning to live with essentials. A surprising 76 percent wanted less emphasis on new goods and services, and more emphasis on "learning to get pleasure out of non-material experiences."

Yet at the same time a *Harvard Business Review* study showed that executives still prefer the traditional ideology of rugged individualism over a more community-oriented philosophy by two and one-half to one, which shows how much our culturally indoctrinated fears block the route to change. Almost three-quarters of the respondents thought a more "communal" ideology would dominate the nation by 1985, yet they themselves found it repugnant. They fear the apparent loss of personal control that they imagine this would bring. When people are threatened they cling to control more violently than ever, even though creative solutions to threat almost always entail *relinquishing* control.

People who try to control and coerce reality to conform to their goals and preconceptions usually find it's a full-time job and not very enjoyable. On the other hand, people who approach life as a stream of events, not to be manipulated but only confronted, tend to have a rich and interesting time of it. For such people, everything that comes along is a potential pathway to be explored—some pleasant, some unpleasant, all valuable. The Ego-dominated wealth addict rejects what is offered by life in favor of the image he has in his head of the reality he wants to bring about. He is the man who can't fully enjoy a movie because he thinks it should have been filmed differently; or who can't fully enjoy a sexual partner because she doesn't conform to some ideal in his head about how the ideal woman should look or act; or who can't enjoy a sunset because he didn't bring a camera; or who can't enjoy a beach because he doesn't own property on it.

The wealth addict has trouble enjoying anything that he can't be sure will be there tomorrow. He hoards during a shortage because he wants to make sure he gets his share before it runs out. A life-loving person can share during a shortage because there are always so many other things in great supply. The wealth addict can't stop looking at what's missing and hence never sees all the other things that have arrived. For a healthy, democratic organism every day brings so many delights and challenges that there is hardly any reason to possess anything.

I have emphasized changing the consciousness of wealth addicts—not because I think this is the most important thing to do, but because it's the thing I can do best. I have not proposed an elaborate set of programs for institutional change because we already have such proposals. We know perfectly well what we need to do, but have lacked the will to do it. Our efforts to transform our condition continually founder on the garish dream of the Closet Addict—the dream of private, exclusive, unshared wealth. My goal is to persuade Americans to repudiate that dream. I don't mean by this that Closet Addicts who are poor should be content with their lot, but rather that their struggle for a better life will be successful only insofar as it is collective. As Hazel Henderson observes, most Americans today are frantically engaged in fighting for first-class cabin space on the Titanic. But the ship still hasn't embarked. I believe there is still time to redirect our energies as a people—to build a society together that will be a source of enjoyment and pride for all of us.

Notes

CHAPTER 1

PAGE
2 Michael Korda's *Success!* (New York: Random House, 1977) and
Power! How to Get It, How to Use It (New York: Random House, 1975),
Martin and Diane Ackerman's *Money, Ego, Power: A Manual for Would-
Be Wheeler-Dealers* (Chicago: Playboy Press, 1976), and Robert
Ringer's *Looking Out for #1* (New York: Fawcett Crest, 1978) and
Winning Through Intimidation (New York: Fawcett Crest, 1975) are
good examples of the more general treatises on how to "make it."
They are only the most recent entries in a long tradition that begins
with Couéism, and continues through Dale Carnegie, Napoleon Hill,
Norman Vincent Peale, Clement Stone, and Leonard Orr. See Dale
Carnegie, *How to Win Friends and Influence People* (New York: Simon
and Schuster, 1947); Napoleon Hill, *Think and Grow Rich* (Meriden,
Conn.: The Ralston Society, 1937); Napoleon Hill and W. Clement
Stone, *Success Through a Positive Mental Attitude* (Englewood Cliffs, N.J.:
Prentice-Hall, 1960); Norman Vincent Peale, *The Power of Positive*

Thinking (Englewood Cliffs, N.J.: Prentice-Hall, 1948); W. Clement Stone, *The Success System That Never Fails* (Englewood Cliffs, N.J.: Prentice-Hall, 1962); and Leonard Orr and Sondra Ray, *Rebirthing in the New Age* (Millbrae, Calif.: Celestial Arts, 1977). They all rely heavily on autosuggestion, and the newer ones of the Korda and Ringer ilk differ only in placing a strong emphasis on ruthless self-centeredness. Books on how to get rich on the stock market are more often of the mail-order variety, too numerous, undistinguished, and undistinguishable to list here. Nothing seems to be more lucrative today than telling other people how to get rich—an irony that seems to be lost on gullible readers. An Ohio man, who publishes a newsletter on magazine and newspaper ads selling moneymaking ideas, observed that after six years of constant inquiry and feedback from readers he has never heard of a single case of anyone making money from such schemes (*Seattle Times,* 4/9/78). The thrust of all these books—that success comes to those who commit themselves totally to these goals —is quite correct. The swindle is that those who are willing to do this don't need the advice, while those who might "profit" from the advice aren't warped enough to take it.

4 Tom Buckley, "Just Plain H. L. Hunt," *Esquire* (January 1967), 148.

6 For a good discussion of the impact of this homogenizing, see Robert L. Heilbroner, *The Quest for Wealth* (New York: Simon and Schuster, 1956), 31–38.

8 *San Francisco Chronicle,* 10/3/76.

15 See Goldian VandenBroeck (ed.), *Less Is More: The Art of Voluntary Poverty* (New York: Harper & Row, 1978) for an excellent compendium of ancient and modern wisdom about money.

CHAPTER 2
PAGE
17–18 See, especially, Sigmund Freud, "Character and Anal Erotism," *Collected Papers,* II (London: Hogarth, 1953); and Ernest Jones, "Anal-Erotic Character Traits," *Journal of Abnormal Psychology,* **13** (1918), 261. See also Ron Kistler, *I Caught Flies for Howard Hughes* (New York: Playboy Press, 1976), 203.

19 C. Wright Mills, *The Power Elite* (New York: Oxford, 1956), 103–

117, and *Power, Politics, and People* (New York: Oxford, 1963), 110–139; see also Ferdinand Lundberg, *The Rich and the Super-Rich* (New York: Lyle Stuart, 1968), Gabriel Kolko, *Wealth and Power in America* (New York: Praeger, 1963), and G. William Domhoff, *The Higher Circles* (New York: Random House, 1970) and *Who Rules America?* (Englewood Cliffs, N.J.: Prentice-Hall, 1967).

24 *San Francisco Chronicle,* 12/27/78.

27 Edmund Bergler, *Money and Emotional Conflicts* (Garden City, N.Y.: Doubleday, 1951), 138.

CHAPTER 3

PAGE

34 Thomas Wiseman, *The Money Motive* (New York: Random House, 1974), 71.

35–36 Harry Hurt III, "Daddy's Money," *Texas Monthly* (April 1978), 184.

40 For a good discussion of Moneythink, its uses, and its dangers, see Michael Phillips, *The Seven Laws of Money* (New York: Random House, 1974), 27 ff.; and Sylvia Porter, *Money Book* (Garden City, N.Y.: Doubleday, 1975).

40 Joseph S. Thorndike, Jr., *The Very Rich: A History of Wealth* (New York: Crown, 1976), 13.

40–41 Phillips, 1 ff.

43 See below, p. 95.

45 Thorndike, 21.

49 Thorndike, 222.

58 *San Francisco Chronicle,* 12/29/78.

61 See Warren G. Bennis and Philip E. Slater, *The Temporary Society* (New York: Harper & Row, 1968), 1–19, 53–76.

CHAPTER 4

PAGE

66 Stewart H. Holbrook, *The Age of the Moguls* (Garden City, N.Y.: Doubleday, 1953), 302, 317–318, 356 ff.

66–67 Arthur M. Louis, "America's Centimillionaires," *Fortune* (May 1968), 155.

68 Peter Collier and David Horowitz, *The Rockefellers* (New York: Holt, Rinehart and Winston, 1976), 6–7, 13; Allan Nevins, *Ford: The Times, The Man, The Company* (New York: Scribner, 1954), 36 ff., 52.

68 Kenneth Lamott, *The Moneymakers: The Great Big New Rich in America* (Boston: Little, Brown, 1969), 294–295.

68 Pitirim Sorokin, "American Millionaires and Multi-Millionaires: A Comparative Statistical Study," *Journal of Social Forces,* III, 4 (May 1925), 633–637.

69 Collier and Horowitz, 12; Lewis Beman, "The Last Billionaires," *Fortune* (November 1976), 132, 135, 226; Cyril Caldwell, *Henry Ford* (New York: Julian Messner, 1947), 9; William Adams Simonds, *Henry Ford: His Life, His Work, His Genius* (New York: Bobbs-Merrill, 1943), 22–23; Lamott, 42, 294–295.

69 Collier and Horowitz, 11.

69–70 Dero A. Saunders, "The Wide Oceans of D. K. Ludwig," *Fortune* (May 1957), 172; Stanley H. Brown, *H. L. Hunt* (Chicago: Playboy Press, 1976), 29 ff.; William Larimer Mellon and Boyden Sparkes, *Judge Mellon's Sons* (privately printed, 1948) 18, 26–30; Harvey O'-Connor, *Mellon's Millions: The Life and Times of Andrew W. Mellon* (New York: Blue Ribbon Books, 1933), 21–22. For more recent biographies of the Mellon family, see Burton Hersh, *The Mellon Family; A Fortune in History* (New York: Morrow, 1978) and David E. Koskoff, *The Mellons: The Chronicle of America's Richest Family* (New York: Crowell, 1978).

70 Jean Paul Getty, *My Life and Fortunes* (New York: Duell, Sloan and Pearce, 1963), 19; Ralph Hewins, *The Richest American: J. Paul Getty* (New York: Dutton, 1960), 16, 41–44, 53, 56.

70 Lamott, 169; Holbrook, 11, 74–75.

71 Thorndike, 15; Max Gunther, *The Very, Very Rich and How They Got That Way* (Chicago: Playboy Press, 1972), 225 ff.; Simonds, 32–35; Albert B. Gerber, *Bashful Billionaire: The Story of Howard Hughes* (New York: Lyle Stuart, 1967), 115–116; Saunders, 172; Collier and Horowitz, 8–13; Brown, 26 ff.; Lamott, 55–56, 169, 254, 265, 294–295.

71–72 Wiseman, 52; *San Francisco Chronicle,* 1/6/78; Brown, 199 (italics added).

72 Thorndike, 168.

72 Brown, 14–15; Lamott, 99.

74 Brown, 50; James Phelan, *Howard Hughes: The Hidden Years* (New York: Random House, 1976), 8, 26, 32–34, 44–49; Kistler, 61–63.

74 Kistler, 191–192.

75 Kistler, 139 ff., 147, 199 ff.

75 See Thorndike, 14; Lamott, 294–295; Goronwy Rees, *The Multimillionaires: Six Studies in Wealth* (New York: Macmillan, 1961), 11–12; Beman, 132.

75 Saunders, 174; Gerber, passim; Brown, 89–90; John B. Rae (ed.), *Henry Ford* (Englewood Cliffs, N.J.: Prentice-Hall, 1969), 106 ff., 127.

76 Lamott, 66; Rees, 7–8, 108 ff., 115 ff.

76–77 Collier and Horowitz, 14, 15, 18, 19, 23–24, 31, 69, 70.

77–78 Caldwell, 35, 37, 40–43, 66 ff., 226; Rae, 35, 45, 51–52, 105–107. See also Anne Jardim, *The First Henry Ford* (Cambridge, Mass.: M.I.T. Press, 1970).

78 Phelan, 39.

78 Rees, 115–116, 124.

78–79 Gunther, 149, 227–228; *Time* (6/13/77); Beman, 134, 226; Lamott, 26–27, 176, 182; Holbrook, 108; Hewins, 16, 80; Brown, 92; Buckley, 152–154; Allan J. Mayer and Annabel Bentley, "The Richest Men in America," *Newsweek* (8/2/76), 56–57.

79 Wiseman, 82–83.

79 O'Connor, 16, 22, 113–114.

79–80 Gunther, 228.

80 Rees, 115, 125.

80 Collier and Horowitz, 32–33.

80–81 Lamott, 28–29; Saunders, 206, 212; Rees, 15; Hewins, 16–18; Holbrook, 108; Mayer and Bentley, 57; Thorndike, 97–98.

81 Lamott, 187, 214; Kistler, 49–50, 151–152; Phelan, 27–30, 69.

81–82 Phelan, 40 ff.; Lamott, 221.

82 Hewins, 19.

82–83 O'Connor, 24.

83 Rees, 9–10, 126.

83 Beman, 135–137; Mayer and Bentley, 57.

83–84 Beman, 226; Saunders, 174 ff.; *Forbes* (4/15/75); *Business Week* (3/21/77).

84 Holbrook, 176.

84–85 Holbrook, 78, 204–205.

85 Brown, 29–32, 43–47, 60–63, 67–74, 93–94, 101–102.

85 Phelan, 36–37, 49–56, 154; Kistler, 28–42, 67–70, 96 ff., 111 ff. See also John Keats, *Howard Hughes* (New York: Random House, 1966), 176–182, 255–264.

85 Lamott, 120, 215–224.

85–86 Lamott, 207–208.

86 Lamott, 240.

88 Lamott, 99, 119–123.

89 Beman, 132–133; Lamott, 273–277, 282; Collier and Horowitz, 412–413. Perhaps the best treatment of this issue can be found in Philip M. Stern's two books: *The Great Treasury Raid* (New York: Random House, 1964) and *The Rape of the Taxpayer* (New York: Random House, 1973).

89 Collier and Horowitz, 41, 43 ff., 56 ff.; Phelan ix ff., 8, 32–34, 69, 75–78, 80, 103.

89–90 Buckley, 68.

90 I won't attempt here to summarize the volumes that have been written on the subject of "taking it from the poor." See, for example, Gustavus Myers, *History of the Great American Fortunes* (New York: Modern Library, 1936); Holbrook; Matthew Josephson, *The Robber Barons* (New York: Harvest Books, 1962).

90 Collier and Horowitz, 402, 419 ff., 566, 588–589; Lamott, 33–38; see also Rae, 75, 109–125.

90 Collier and Horowitz, 109–115, 123.

91 Holbrook, 9–10.

91–92 Wiseman, 31 ff.

92 Lamott, 110.

92 Lamott, 96–123.

92–93 Wiseman, 127.

93 Holbrook, 9–10, 78–79, 271; Lamott, 99, 104, 110; Rees, 5–6.

93–94 Holbrook, 20–21, 56, 215; Lamott, 94–95, 104, 294–295; O'-Connor 24; Collier and Horowitz, 11, 14.

94 *Wall Street Journal,* 4/13/79; *San Francisco Chronicle,* 4/17/79, 4/22/79 through 4/27/79; *TIME,* 6/13/77.

94–95 *TIME,* 6/13/77.

95 Rees, 117 ff.; Lamott, 12, 19, 237; Caldwell, 232–233; Buckley, 148; Thorndike, 13; Gunther, 71.

95 Gunther, 71, 198; Simonds, 27–28; Caldwell, 44, 55–57; Rae, 5, 8, 72–74, 107, 114–122, 128–129, 154–155, 175–179.

95–96 Holbrook, 77; Thorndike, 305–306, 330.

96 *Boston Globe,* 5/30/78.

96–97 Brown, 175; Hurt, 185; Lamott, 204 ff.; Rae, 76–77; Rees, 17, 120–121; Collier and Horowitz, 471–474, 619–620.

97 Louis, *Fortune,* 196; Brown, 10; Buckley, 64, 146, 152; Lamott, 187, 206, 238; Rees, 108.

97–98 T. A. Wise, "The Incorrigible John MacArthur," *Fortune* (July 1958), 129; Phelan, ix–xiii, 32; Holbrook, 349.

98 Bergler, 145–146; Thorndike, 48; Lamott, 192–195; Collier and Horowitz, 69–70; Wiseman, 113–114. See also Beman, 134; Lamott, 175, 243–245.

98–99 Thorndike, 24, 176–177; Lamott, 186; Collier and Horowitz, 84–85, 91–92; Holbrook, 340–343.

99 *TIME,* 6/13/77.

100 Wiseman, 56–57; Collier and Horowitz, 45–46.

100 Holbrook, 212–213; Rees, 17.

100–101 Phelan, 4–5, 19–20, 45, 58 ff., 115, 180; Kistler, 102 ff., 121; *TIME,* 12/13/76.

101 Gunther, 215, 227; Thorndike, 16; Rees, 114–119; Hewins, 19.

See also Mayer and Bentley, 56; Saunders, 216; Phelan, 32, 42; Buckley, 142; Lamott, 251–266; Holbrook, 134; John Cuber and Peggy Harroff, *Sex and the Significant Americans* (Baltimore, Md.: Penguin Books, 1965), 172–180.

101 *TIME,* 6/13/77; Buckley, 66; Hewins, 41, 53–54, 97–99, 126.

102 Gunther, 226; Phelan, 3, 92, 181–182; Kistler, 116–118, 131–133.

102–103 Robert Coles, "Children of Affluence," *Atlantic Monthly* (September 1977), 55 ff.; Michael H. Stone and Clarice J. Kestenbaum, "Maternal Deprivation in Children of the Wealthy," *History of Childhood Quarterly* (Summer 1974), 96–98; Roy R. Grinker, Jr., "The Poor Rich," *Psychology Today* (October 1977), 74 ff.; *Newsweek,* 8/29/77; Michael H. Stone, "Treating the Wealthy and Their Children," *International Journal of Child Psychotherapy* **I,** 15–46.

103 *Newsweek,* 8/29/77; Coles, *Atlantic,* 55, 57, 58–59; Grinker, 75.

103 Thorndike, 331; Louis, 195. See also Alvin Moscow, *The Rockefeller Inheritance* (Garden City, N.Y.: Doubleday, 1977).

103–104 Coles, *Atlantic,* 63–64; Collier and Horowitz, 303; Sorokin, 639–640; Thorndike, 335; see also Stone and Kestenbaum, 96; Phillips, 88 ff., 95 ff.

104 See John W. Tebbel, *The Inheritors: A Study of America's Great Fortunes and What Happened to Them* (New York: Putnam, 1962); and Robert Coles, *Privileged Ones: The Well-Off and the Rich in America* (Boston: Little, Brown, 1978).

104 Collier and Horowitz, 525; see also 505 ff., 508, 525–529, 535, 591–593, 615.

104–105 Grinker, 81.

105 Holbrook, 214–215; O'Connor, 20, 111.

105 Hurt, 181–182, 196–202; see also Brown, 10 ff.

105–106 Grinker, 75; Mellon and Sparkes, 26–28.

106 Hurt, 96, 181–182; Brown, 1–2, 160, 187.

106 Rae, 8; Caldwell, 221; Allan Nevins and Frank Ernest Hill, *Ford: Decline and Rebirth, 1933–1962* (New York: Scribner, 1962), 115–117, 240–248.

106–107 Hurt, 182–184; Brown, 154; see also, Wiseman, 91–92.

107–108 Lamott, 202; Phelan, 89; O'Connor, 338.

108 Phelan, 177; Keats, 5; Rae, 103–105, 150; Nevins and Hill, 231–239.

108 Collier and Horowitz, 47.

108 Louis, 195; Wiseman, 223–224; see also Gunther, 226; Bergler, 58.

109 Phelan, 24, 43.

109 Phelan, 17 ff., 38 ff.; Hewins, 78–81, 129.

109 Phelan, 38, 102–104.

109–110 Phelan, 125–137, 143–144, 149–150.

110 Rees, 110–112.

110 Rae, 84.

111 W. Lloyd Warner and James Abegglen, *Big Business Leaders in America* (New York: Harper, 1955), 64–83; Hewins, 16, 39, 50, 134, 232. See also Jean Paul Getty, *As I See It* (Englewood Cliffs, N.J.: Prentice-Hall, 1976), 88.

111–112 Simonds, 23, 32–34; Caldwell, 12; Nevins, 43, 49–51; Jardim, 158–180, esp. 161.

112 Brown, 17–19; Holbrook, 11, 76; Donald L. Bartlett and James B. Steele, *Empire: The Life, Legend, and Madness of Howard Hughes* (New York: Norton, 1979), 38–45.

113 Bergler, 42 ff., 56–57, 62.

CHAPTER 5
PAGE

123 Scott Burns, *Home Inc.* (Garden City, N.Y.: Doubleday, 1975).

124–125 *San Francisco Chronicle*, 7/14/76; Thorndike, 12, 289 ff., 304 ff.; *San Francisco Chronicle*, 11/15/78.

125 *San Francisco Chronicle*, 11/15/78.

125–126 *San Francisco Chronicle*, 12/27/78; Hugh Drummond, "Dr. Drummond on the Big Casino," *Mother Jones* (December 1977) and "Pocketa Pocketa Machines," *Mother Jones* (January 1978).

128–129 See, for example, *San Francisco Chronicle,* 11/22/78; *Omni* (March 1979) 40.

129 Collier and Horowitz, 234–323, esp. 273, 294 ff., and 326 ff., 339, 343–344, 402, 418–420.

CHAPTER 6
PAGE
131 Lamott, 13–14.

132 Lundberg, 13, 17; David Caplovitz, *The Poor Pay More: Consumer Practices of Low-Income Families* (New York: Free Press, 1967).

132–133 *Boston Globe,* 5/7/78; *San Francisco Chronicle,* 2/13/78; Lamott, 271, 288.

133 *Boston Globe,* 3/27/78; Lamott, 272 ff.; Wiseman, 129.

136 Hugh Drummond, "Your Health at Too High a Premium," *Mother Jones* (May 1977).

137 *San Francisco Examiner,* 5/5/76; Ramón Margalef, "Perspectives in Ecological Theory," *CoEvolution Quarterly* (Summer 1975), 58–61.

137–138 *San Francisco Chronicle,* 7/8/78.

138 Hurt, 198.

140 *San Francisco Chronicle,* 2/7/76.

141 *Mother Jones* (November 1978), 54–66.

141 See, for example, *San Francisco Chronicle,* 10/24/78, 11/14/78, 3/29/79, *Mother Jones* (April 1977) and (August 1977).

142 Lundberg, 13, 17.

142 Jack Anderson, *San Francisco Chronicle,* 7/6/78.

143 Collier and Horowitz, 66 ff., 100 ff., 104 ff., 143, 490–492, 661–663, 665–667.

144 Thorndike, 24; Collier and Horowitz, 615.

144–145 See Thorndike, 335; John Curtis Raines, *Illusions of Success* (Valley Forge, Penn.: Judson Press, 1975).

146 See, for example, Holbrook, 133–134, 143; Collier and Horowitz, 52, 62–63, 102 ff.; and Sigmund Diamond, *The Reputation of the American Businessman* (New York: Harper & Row, 1966).

147 Collier and Horowitz, 109 ff., 114–115, 123.

147 O'Connor, 207–226; see also Nevins and Hill, 111–115, 133–167.

CHAPTER 7
PAGE
156–157 Lamott, 283–286.

157 For more detail on this point, see *The Pursuit of Loneliness,* rev. ed. (Boston: Beacon Press, 1976), 168–202.

160–161 See, for example, VandenBroeck, *Less Is More,* passim.

161–162 Marshall Sahlins, *Stone Age Economics* (Chicago: Aldine, 1972), 1–39.

162 Percival Goodman and Paul Goodman. *Communitas* (New York: Vintage Books, 1960), 188–194.

162 *San Francisco Chronicle,* 11/30/78.

175 Psychoanalysts like to refer to this aspect of the despotic Ego as the "superego." I regard the "superego" as a conceptual red herring invented by the Ego Mafia to make the despotic Ego appear more benign than it really is. Psychoanalysis as a movement has always been fundamentally on the side of the Ego-despot, painting the Constituents in dark and frightening colors and offering only the minimum degree of democratic reform necessary to solidify the Ego's rigid control.

177 It has become fashionable in the last few years to trash the Human Potential Movement (see Christopher Lasch, *The Culture of Narcissism* [New York: Norton, 1978] and Peter Marin, "The New Narcissism," *Harper's* [October 1975], 45–56, for the most serious of these efforts), and I don't want my remarks on hedonism to be taken as an attempt to join the horde. There are many flaws and absurdities in any new movement, but I find it highly suspicious when people attack as "narcissistic" a sincere and often successful attempt at democratization of the organism. Our whole culture rests on narcissism, as I have tried to show elsewhere (See *Earthwalk* [Garden City, N.Y.: Anchor Press, 1974]) and this affects even attempts to change it. It surprises me that people who could swallow the kind of narcissism that created the horrors of modern warfare, the monstrosities of

technology, and the gross inequities in wealth and power that dominate our society, could strain at the gnat of Esalen or *est.* In all this
anxiety about the "new" narcissism it isn't hard to detect the Ego's
fear that the old narcissism might be abandoned. The efforts of the
Human Potential Movement to reduce the despotism of the Ego and
give more power to the Constitutents are often confused, muddle-
headed and self-defeating, but they are attempts. The slave may sneer
when he sees the freedman showing remnants of his old habits of
deference, but is he sneering at the part that's still enslaved or at the
part that's free?

184 James, *The Varieties of Religious Experience* (quoted in VandenBroeck, 84).

184–185 Duane Elgin and Arnold Mitchell, "Voluntary Simplicity
(3)," *CoEvolution Quarterly* (Summer 1977), 5–8.

185 VandenBroeck, 4.

186 Richard Gregg, "Voluntary Simplicity (1)," *CoEvolution Quarterly*
(Summer 1977), 27.

187 Elgin and Mitchell, 4, 10–12.

192 Illich, *Energy and Equity* (quoted in Tom Bender, "Why We Need
to Get Poor Quick," *The Futurist* [August 1977], 212).

193 Elgin and Mitchell, 5–8.

193–194 *San Francisco Chronicle,* 2/15/78.

196 Wiseman, 53–54.

196–197 Duane Elgin and Arnold Mitchell, "Voluntary Simplicity:
Life-Style of the Future?" *The Futurist* (August 1977), 209.

197 Elgin and Mitchell, *CQ,* 11.

198 Hazel Henderson, *Creating Alternative Futures* (New York: Berkley
Windhover, 1978), 7. This book does a superb job of exposing the
absurd premises and fundamental vacuity of most current economic
thinking.